THE DEFINITIVE QUOTE-TO-CASH GUIDE

EVERYTHING YOU WANTED TO KNOW ABOUT QUOTE-TO-CASH BUT WERE AFRAID TO ASK

Gilles Muys

ISBN-978-1-945431-16-6

Printed in the United States of America

TABLE OF CONTENTS

FOREWORD

I first met Gilles at Dreamforce 2012. SteelBrick had a tiny booth in the back of the expo, and I staffed the booth every one of the open hours back then. So Gilles and I had to meet during a break in the expo for Marc Benioff's keynote. Phillip Smith, who had joined me as the first account executive earlier in the year, recommended I speak with Gilles. They had met earlier at the Cloud CPQ pioneer BigMachines, where they both worked. Phillip said Gilles is brilliant and, boy, was he right!

Gilles started to work with us part-time at first, but I quickly realized he was too good not to hire full-time. I bootstrapped the business and had no money. But I knew I couldn't afford to pass on Gilles. In the next year, we grew our install base to well over 100 happy customers, crossed $1M in ARR, and attracted outside capital from the founding team at BigMachines. I can confidently say we couldn't achieve any of those milestones had it not been for Gilles' expertise, passion, and dedication.

CPQ was too difficult and too expensive to deploy and maintain in 2006. SteelBrick CPQ was built to change that. The idea was to democratize this important technology by building on a market-leading CRM platform and, more importantly, following Salesforce's mantra of "clicks, not code." Our vision was validated when Salesforce acquired SteelBrick in 2016 and ultimately grew Salesforce CPQ into the market leader, with close to 4,000 customers—more than every other CPQ vendor combined!

Gilles Muys is the world's foremost expert on this ground-breaking product. Since I partnered with Gilles, he has implemented or architected close to a thousand CPQ projects. He quite possibly knows the product better than me—and I built the darn thing. The words of wisdom and practical advice he shares in this book are a must-read for any aspiring CPQ architect, admin, or stakeholder. There is no substitute for experience in CPQ projects, and I can't think of anyone more experienced than Gilles!

MAX RUDMAN, Founder of SteelBrick and Prodly CEO

Gilles Muys was a key member of our team as we pioneered the quote-to-cash industry over the past 20 years. First at BigMachines (now Oracle CPQ cloud) and then at SteelBrick (now Salesforce CPQ and Billing), Gilles was a core member and leader of our technical solutions teams.

At SteelBrick, Gilles was the third employee, and he worked very closely with founder/CTO Max Rudman to architect the SteelBrick solution on top of Salesforce to elegantly fulfill complex customer needs.

As a former CFO, Gilles brought in-depth financial and business knowledge, which he combined with his stellar technical acumen to bring a unique, in-depth understanding of both the business processes and systems required to automate configuring, pricing, quoting, ordering, and billing products in a B2B environment.

Gilles' depth of knowledge—something gained only through years of hard work successfully deploying hundreds of quote-to-cash solutions—is encapsulated here in this comprehensive quote-to-cash guide An in-depth look at the processes that comprise quote-to-cash (i.e., contract lifecycle management, configuration, pricing, quoting, and billing), this book has come at the right time. I highly recommend it to anyone seeking to learn more about quote-to-cash process improvement.

Whether you're a CEO, a salesperson, an accountant, or someone just trying to understand the sales cycle better, I promise that you'll never see sales the same way again.

GODARD ABEL, G2 CEO and Former SteelBrick CEO

INTRODUCTION

There is a fundamental truth of the business world—something as great and inevitable as death and taxes—and it's a hard pill to swallow: It doesn't matter how revolutionary or world-changing an idea is: without sales, that idea will die.

This truth is not exclusive to salespeople. The sales process is much more inclusive than that. It involves everyone—from the CEO to a member of the accounting department. Everyone in the organization has some role to play. And that means everyone should take an interest in quote-to-cash.

Quote-to-cash, or QTC, refers to the integration and automated management of end-to-end business processes involved in selling. It is the foundation on which we build revenue, designed to simplify and accelerate the sales process. And this foundation includes other acronyms as well: CRM (customer relationship management) software is vital for managing customer data and moving leads and opportunities down the sales funnel. CPQ (configure, price, quote) platforms enable salespeople to automate the quoting process with greater speed and accuracy. ERP (enterprise resource planning) tools manage billing, inventory, and resources across the organization.

These tools (and many others) perform vital business functions that help turn those great ideas into viable businesses. Using quote-to-cash, companies experience the following:

- 105 percent increase in deal size
- 38 percent faster sales cycle
- 200 percent increase in conversions

Further, with a fully executed quote-to-cash system, you'll be able to do the following:

- Increase the productivity of your sales teams and back-office functions by automating sales processes
- Optimize quoting and discounting to improve profit margins
- Increase revenue by pointing sales to opportunities for cross-selling complementary products and services
- Create efficient, accurate, and tailored sales processes that improve the sales experience
- Enhance your brand, improve conversion ratios, and gain more opportunities for repeat business
- Streamline processes while ensuring that sales teams are meeting company compliance policies and regulatory requirements

As the global leader in quote-to-cash, Simplus is uniquely qualified to guide you and your company through all aspects of the journey. As part of our mission to do so, I have written this book—a roadmap of quote-to-cash—to get you ready for the work ahead. In general, we'll be asking and answering three questions about quote-to-cash:

PART 1: What is quote-to-cash, and what does it entail?

PART 2: Where does quote-to-cash fit in the overall business process?

PART 3: What best practices should I follow to ensure a successful quote-to-cash journey?

Remember this: you are not alone in your quote-to-cash journey. This book will serve as your map, and Simplus is standing at the ready to step in as your guide. So read on, take a survey of the terrain, and let us know when you're ready to embark. We'll get through this together.

PART ONE

WHAT IS QUOTE-TO-CASH?

CHAPTER ONE

CPQ

In 2015, Accenture found that 83 percent of companies surveyed were using tools for CPQ. According to Salesforce, the CPQ market is projected to maintain a steady 20 percent annual growth through 2020.[1] What is it about CPQ that makes it so popular among professionals, and at an ever-increasing rate at that? And is it time for you, if you haven't already, to jump on the bandwagon?

CPQ stands for "Configure Price Quote," the first component of the giant that is quote-to-cash.

Let's examine each step of the process individually and then as a whole.

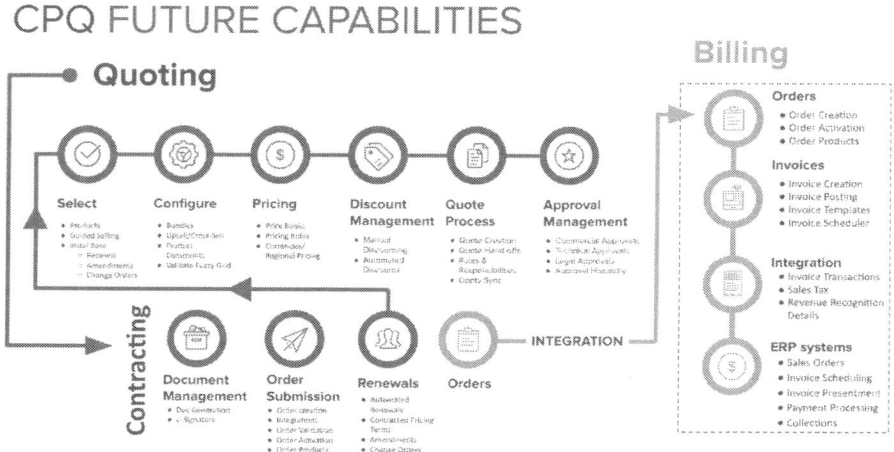

Configuration

Configuration is the process of first understanding and then packaging your products and services in order to sell them together so that they represent an effective solution to address your end customer's requests and needs. Besides considering the products and services that intuitively complement one another, look for exclusions, dependencies, and other constraints.

Exclusions

Imagine you were buying a car and needed to choose an engine model to go with it. The car only has room for one engine, so you wouldn't be able to purchase both a V6 and a V8 engine for the same vehicle. We can therefore say that these two engines are "not compatible with each other," and you must choose one and only one of them for your particular car. In a similar way, you need to look at your offerings and determine how they do and do not work together. Which of your products and services are incompatible with one another? Are there any internal policies or domestic/international regulations keeping some products or services from being sold in certain regions?

Dependencies

Let's go back to the car you're considering buying. You wouldn't be able to buy insurance for that car before buying the car itself, nor would you be able to buy larger tires without buying appropriate wheels first. Likewise, dependencies are those products or services that hinge on the purchase of other offerings. Understanding or dictating these dependencies will allow you to bundle them with their corresponding offerings. It's also a chance to upsell: if a user were to select an item in the product catalog that can't be sold on its own, you could prohibit the item from being added to the quote without also selecting the appropriate offerings.

Quantity-Based Constraints

In any business, a quantity-based constraint is one that restricts the sale of a product if a certain quantity-based condition isn't met. For example, when you finally get around to buying that car, you'll need tires to go with it. You won't need more than four or five, though, and the dealership isn't going to let you leave with more than will fit on your vehicle. If you are keen on buying spare tires just in case, they would be sold separately as spare parts, not as part of your vehicle.

Configuration can quickly become complex for your sales reps, so automation in this step is vital. Offer your sales reps guided configuration—by asking a series of questions, the automated system can handle some or all of the configuration, identifying the exclusions, dependencies, and quantity-based constraints, quickly and without error. The end goal is to quote a solution that is technically and commercially viable to your end clients, so everything you can do to empower your sales reps to deliver the right solution to your clients is worth your time and attention.

Pricing

With configuration out of the way, the time has come to price your selected offering. Though vital to your processes, pricing has the potential to include complex calculations. While pricing methods vary, all can benefit from a consistent rhyme and reason, which can be enforced and strengthened by automation. Human beings tend to be very creative in determining how a "special price" can help us close a deal, but at the end of the day, most pricing approaches follow a core set of models.

Pricing Methods

There is no one right way to price your offerings. Here are some of the most common pricing methods used across different industries. (Keep in mind that some of these methods can be combined.)

- **List Pricing:** This is the most simple, direct approach to pricing. With this pricing method, you pull a reference price—sometimes called "standard price," "list price," or "MSRP"—from a central table or price book.

- **Cost + Markup:** This method is most commonly used by resellers or by manufacturers. You determine the price of the product by taking its cost (this is often your purchase price from your supplier, or it could be your own manufacturing cost) and adding a markup. You determine the markup by calculating the profit margin you try to achieve.

- **Attribute-Based Pricing:** In attribute-based pricing, businesses vary the price of a product based on the value of one or more attributes of the product. For example, maybe you sell articles of clothing at different prices depending on each article's size (small, medium, etc.). Taken further, maybe you allow your client to choose the fabric or material used to make a product, with each option coming at a different price. This method can quickly become complex as you increase the number of price-relevant attributes. Or, it can simplify your product catalog: a single entry in the catalog can represent multiple variants of the product based on how the sales rep sets the value of each attribute of the product.

- **Block Pricing:** With block pricing, you sell a group of identical products by "buckets" of quantity, with one specific price for the entire bucket. Block pricing is therefore a form of tiered pricing. Think of buying minutes for your cell phone plan or a box of new business cards. In this model, you are not using a price per unit. Instead, you sell with a price for the entire bucket. Whether or not you use all of the minutes or give out all of your business cards, the purchase price does not change. For end customers, the average purchase price per unit is based on their consumption.

- **Customer-Specific Pricing:** Sometimes, a customer gets special treatment. In negotiations, you may offer and agree upon a discounted price for your customer. As this is not your standard price, it will often be valid only for a set period of time, based on the expected volume of business you expect your customer to do with you.

- **Percent of Total:** The percent-of-total method, sometimes called "dynamic pricing," involves calculating a product's list price using a percentage of the total price of one or several other products. For example, if you are selling a software license, you may charge a support service for 20 percent of the price of the license.

- **Term Pricing:** Sometimes, the list price may vary depending on the term of the contract you have with your end customers. You may, for example, offer a 10 percent discount if your client commits for a two-year contract, and 20 percent for a three-year contract. Accordingly, term pricing is commonly applied to recurring revenue products and services.

- **Volume Pricing:** Volume pricing is similar to block pricing in that it represents a form of tiered pricing. However, contrary to block pricing, this is a price per unit approach, with a price that varies based on the quantity sold. Note that you can sometimes use a different unit of measure in lieu of quantity to determine your tiers. There are different variants of volume pricing in this regard, and the most common approach is to apply a discount to your list price that varies based on the volume purchased by your client.

Attribute-Based Pricing Considerations

If you plan to rationalize and simplify your product catalog (i.e., reduce the number of SKUs) by introducing attribute-based pricing, you need to carefully consider how your attribute-based pricing model will be designed. There are two main approaches to this problem.

The first approach is to create a lookup table where you will create a record for each combination of attribute values and assign a specific price for that combination. This often leads to a single lookup table with a large number of records. These records will need to be maintained. In essence, you have moved your product catalog maintenance burden from a product table with separate SKUs per combination of attribute values to a lookup table that stores the price for each combination of attribute values. In other words, you have moved your pain point to a different place.

The second approach is to assign a price adjustment factor to each value of each attribute and then use a formula to dynamically calculate the price. For example, your small shirt has an adjustment factor of 0.8, the medium shirt a factor of 1, and the large shirt a factor of 1.1. Independently from the size attribute, you also assign an adjustment factor for the type of material: fabric has a factor of 1, and leather has a factor of 2. You then apply these adjustment factors to the "base price" of the product, which itself is stored in your price book. Your final formula might then look like this:

```
Base Price x Size Adjustment Factor x Material Adjustment Factor
```

In this example, you only have to maintain two very small lookup tables: size attribute with only three values, and material attribute with only two values. An important point here is that you can shape that formula any way you want or need: instead of using adjustment factors in a multiplication operation, you could use amount-based factors and additions, such as this:

```
Base Price + Price Impact of Size + Price Impact of Material
```

Therefore, you have a lot of flexibility, as you can also easily mix and match the types of operations to get to the most appropriate price for your business, your industry, your geography, and so on.

In the context of a large number of different attributes, the second approach will generate a much simpler solution and a significantly lower maintenance cost.

As you go through your digital transformation journey, keep simplicity in mind. Contrary to common belief, complexity is often manufactured. You have the power to choose the opposite path of simplicity.

Consistency Is Key

Whatever method or mixture of methods you use, consistency is key. As Dan Lindsey, director of sales and business development at SupplyKick, explains,

> Your brand's reputation is also at risk in the eyes of potential customers. If a product that sells for $100 in-store is regularly found on Amazon for $65, and the presentation of the item is varied and inconsistent, shoppers may become wary of the product's quality. As much as everyone loves a great deal, consumers also want to be sure that the product meets the expectations the brand has established across retail outlets.[2]

Now, that doesn't mean that you have one fixed price with no room for negotiation. No matter what pricing model you use, you're still bound to come across exceptions, be they promotional discounts, add-ons, etc. But these exceptions need to have clear and consistent processes to them—processes that are easily understood by your sales reps and customers alike.

But maybe you fear that consistency must be sacrificed in the face of complexity. Not at all. Even a complex pricing method can be consistent. This consistency will give you more opportunities to automate price calculations. With automated pricing processes, you can be certain that your prices are consistently accurate and lead to more predictable margins.

Take Centrify, for example. The company's price book was thick: it wasn't that Centrify had an enormous product catalog. Rather, those products came in a wide array of combinations, with different offerings, subscriptions, etc., adding up to around 2,000 items. All those possibilities made pricing quickly and accurately difficult. Mark Gremban, senior sales operations manager at Centrify, says,

> We were forcing our reps to make a decision based on this long list of [products]. You know, people are people—we make mistakes. A sales rep would accidentally select a SKU for a two-year subscription instead of the three-year requested by the customer, or a standard service level instead of a premium service level. It was really just becoming a problem on the backend.[3]

Moving to an automated CPQ process fixed those problems for Centrify. Rather than forcing sales reps to meticulously work out the price on their own, the new system automatically generated the price, streamlining the process and satisfying customers faster than ever before.

Your best approach to automate pricing is to understand the capabilities of your CPQ platform and align your pricing models and pricing policies to what is supported out of the box as much as possible. You should look at this problem from a holistic perspective as well, not just from a pure pricing point of view. For example, if your company offers tiered pricing, recognize that tiered pricing models such as volume discounts correspond to pricing policies established by your company. Your sales hierarchy should not have to approve volume discounts unless they are specific to the end customer you are quoting for and represent a departure from the standard volume discount for a product or service. Taking this a step further, do you really need a different volume discount structure for that end customer, or can you close the deal with a more traditional discretionary discount?

You can make your policies, and therefore your CPQ solution, as simple or as complex as you want. Avoid manufacturing complexity in your business processes, and take advantage of out-of-the-box functionality from CPQ. In CPQ, adjusting your processes to your tool can be a tremendous advantage.

Price Waterfall

The price waterfall is the mathematical representation of how you go from a list price to a net price. It involves applying different types of discounts progressively.

Your company should have a clear discounting policy for every type of discount. The most commonly found discounts are the following:

- **Discretionary Discount:** Manually entered by the sales rep, although it can be defaulted or controlled by the system.
- **Volume Discount:** Progressive discount offered to a client based on the volume of business they do with you, traditionally through the use of tiers. (In most cases, the volume is measured via the quantity of the item, but it could be a different unit of measure not related to quantity. There are different types of algorithms to calculate this type of discount.)
- **Term Discount:** Progressive discount offered to a client for a recurring revenue product or service, based on the term (duration) of the contract that this client is willing to commit to.
- **Channel Discounts:** Discount offered to a partner or a distributor in the context of channel sales.

- **Industry Discount:** Discount offered to a client in a specific vertical. Note that NFP (not for profit) discounts usually operate under the same logic.
- **Promotions:** Discounts offered on a temporary basis.

The price waterfall needs to document precisely how all these discounts work together and how they are calculated, either cumulatively or in a cascading manner. You also need to document what is the price point used to apply the discount.

Ultimately, your CPQ solution needs to be designed and implemented to support your documented price waterfall. Once again, the more consistent you are between all your products, the easier it will be to configure and maintain your product catalog and your pricing logic to apply the expected waterfall.

Quote

Quote presentment is usually the easiest aspect of CPQ. It can be broken down into four steps: approval, document generation, client acceptance, and (by extension of acquiring a new client) amendments and renewals.

1. Approval

Before your quote can be accepted by the client, it should go through internal approval. Just like in pricing, you are in control of the level of complexity of this process. Some companies fail to enforce simplification by allowing varied approval processes (e.g., having different discount approval structures that vary by region, product family, and client markets). Doing so only makes the process more complicated for you, your CPQ administrator, and your quoting users. To eliminate confusion and streamline quoting, the internal approval process should be uniform across your entire company. More standardization means greater ease in implementing and automating the approval process. Therefore, think twice before confirming that you absolutely need a complex process.

An important factor in knowing if you have simplified enough is evaluating the maximum number of approvers involved in the most complex quote. You should target a maximum of five to seven approvers. Beyond this threshold, you will likely promote a longer sales cycle, which leads to lost deals and the perception by your clients that it's difficult to do business with you.

The most common approval reasons are summarized as follows:

- **Pricing approval:** For decisions based on discount level, margin, or deal size.
- **Finance approval:** For payment terms or billing terms, for example.
- **Legal approval:** If you allow custom terms and conditions to be specified on a quote-per-quote basis.
- **Product-specific approvals:** When an approval is required if a product is quoted regardless of its price or discount.

Once you have determined the reasons for which a quote should be approved, optimize your approval cycle by taking advantage of triggering your approvals in parallel. Another important consideration is to implement smart approvals: In this case, after a quote has first been rejected, a sales rep will modify the quote to address the feedback from the approver who rejected it and resubmit for approval. With smart approvals, the system will not seek approval a second time for what was already approved in the first submission.

Salesforce CPQ offers a powerful Advanced Approvals module that supports such advanced functionality.

> **TIP:** As your sales reps work pricing in the quote, think about including a visual indicator for the level of approval that will be required, especially for pricing approvals. If they see a red indicator (meaning the VP or CEO will have to approve), they will likely rethink the level of discount they have applied to the quote. Such visual indicators have proven to have a significant influence on the behavior of sales reps and can contribute to increasing margin levels.

2. Document Generation

Once the quote has been approved internally, it can be forwarded to the client. For that to happen, though, you need a physical or digital document.

Document generation can take advantage of dynamic templates. A good document-generation engine should offer you the flexibility to meet the complexity of business transactions. You will need tools that allow you to dynamically group or sort products and services, automatically show or hide information based on contextual data, or generate a dynamic set of terms and conditions that match the products and services quoted to each specific client. You will need tools accounting for localization concerns (e.g., language, symbols, etc.) That's not to mention aesthetics, as you will need as much control as possible over your documents' layout as well as their general look and feel.

Additionally, you'll want to make sure your document takes branding into consideration. The quote document is a selling tool—not just a set of products with an agreed-upon price.

Here are some best practices for quotes that will stand out and sell with your company branding:

- Use a company style guide to design the quote document (e.g., company-approved graphics and color themes). You want to make the document feel as much a part of your business as any other client-facing content without overwhelming it with design elements.

- Organize the document and ensure it is easily legible. That will save you time spent on the phone explaining the document to your client.

- Present the information as clearly and concisely as possible. The quote document is a rhetorical, persuasive document, and it reflects on your business—if it is difficult to understand, your client may think that working with you will be difficult as well.

- Decide whether you will have a quick output including only a price sheet, a complete proposal that presents company information, or a combination of the two. In general, the complete proposal is best for new clients, and the quick price sheet works best for repeat customers.

- When it comes to pricing information, make sure you include all the necessary elements for your client to verify your math. Most clients recompute the quote total by multiplying quantity and unit price for each product, verifying discount levels and calculations, and checking the corresponding totals for groups of products and the entire quote.

- Personalize the quote document by including an optional cover page or personalized cover letter designed by the sales rep. Remember: your business is all about people.

While CPQ and automation can do a lot, it is up to you to maintain trust and build relationships.

By using a powerful document engine, you will be able to automate the generation of different types of documents based on the contextual information from the quote, the client account, or other criteria of your choice. As always, try not to overengineer your quote templates. Sometimes, it's better to have two different but simple templates, rather than a single but complex one.

3. Client Acceptance

Client acceptance can only come about through negotiation, which begins the moment you send the quote output to the client. Your job is to make it as easy as possible for the client to review, sign, and return the quote to you as quickly as possible. Ideally, every document you send your client should allow for electronic signature; not only is it more convenient than demanding your clients find and use a fax machine, but it also allows you to track metadata about the signature process and trigger other business processes. For example, when the system detects electronic acceptance, it can automatically close/win the opportunity, generate one or several orders for fulfillment, and complete the contracting process.

The negotiation process includes more than agreeing on products and services or their prices. It can also deal with reviewing and adjusting the terms and conditions of sale, commonly known as the "redlining process." Redlining is not part of CPQ. Therefore, if you have a need for redlining, be sure to read chapter 2 about CLM (contract lifecycle management). CLM tools are designed to efficiently support the redlining process, among other numerous benefits.

4. Amendments and Renewals

Once the client has accepted the quote, several important processes are triggered.

The first one is fulfillment, and we will come back to it later in chapter 5.

The second critical process is to create your end customer's installed base and is commonly known as the "contracting" process. This installed base is a record of all products and services purchased by the customer; it is the base for triggering the next steps in your sales cycle. CPQ is a heavy consumer of this data, which must be accurate at all times.

This is a complex process that should be handled out-of-the-box by your CPQ platform with available automation points, especially if you are in a recurring revenue model. Products or services that are sold as one-time transactions are converted into assets, while recurring products or services are converted into subscriptions. Whenever you deal with subscriptions, an important mind shift is critical: your transactions are no longer "frozen in time," and they follow a lifecycle of their own because there is now a time element attached to these products and services. During the term of the transaction or contract, your customer might want to amend the contract (e.g., add or remove products and services, cancel or terminate them), and you hope that they will renew their business at the end of the term.

- **Amendment:** A transaction that modifies the products or services purchased before the end date of the contract
- **Renewal:** Products and services that are purchased again (i.e., renewed, once the contract expires)

From a best practice perspective, think about the following key automation points:

- Upon creation of the contract and the installed base information or shortly thereafter, automatically create your future renewal opportunity. This will give your business better visibility into the future.

- When getting close to the term of the contract, generate a renewal quote. If your renewal sales cycle is 30 days, generate the renewal quote 30 days before the end of the contract and notify the sales rep so that they can start working the renewal with their customer.

- Amendments typically occur between the two above events. The products and services added to the contract through these amendments should become part of the future renewal. Therefore, it's important that your CPQ platform automatically update the renewal opportunity accordingly.

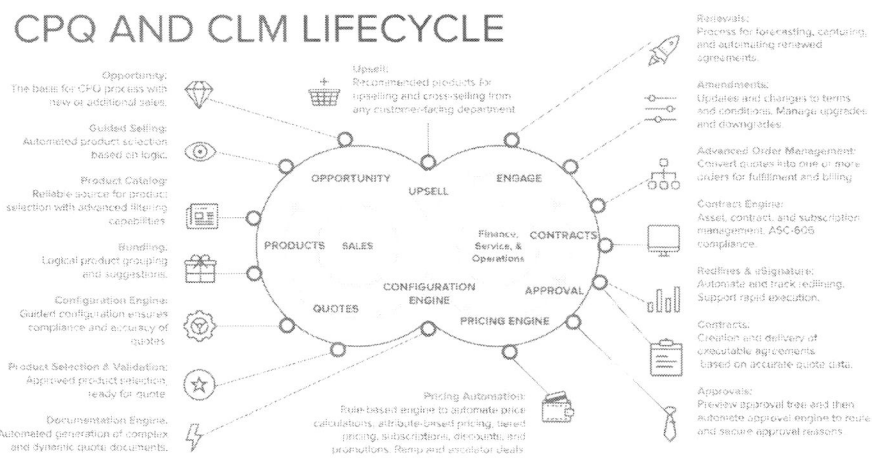

CPQ AND CLM LIFECYCLE

Pain Points

Now you know what CPQ is and what each part of the solution stands for. But how does all this relate to the day-to-day challenges your business is facing? Here are some of the common pain points we notice among most companies:

- Juggling multiple and disparate pricing data sources
- Lengthy quote-generation time
- Time-consuming reporting tasks
- Lack of visibility or control into the sales cycle
- Selling technically incorrect sets of products and services that can't be delivered
- Repeating pricing errors
- Excessive discount levels
- Missed opportunities on renewal business
- Missing add-on and upsell opportunities
- Sales reps burdened with administrative tasks and poor productivity
- Business silos slowing down the sales cycle
- Inconsistent quote presentment and lost opportunity to sell
- Lack of team collaboration
- Lengthy approval cycles
- Scattered or tribal knowledge with no reference source
- Extremely manual processes, manipulating (mostly outdated) spreadsheets, text documents, and emails
- No central repository for products, pricing, and quoting information
- Unused data

How CPQ Helps

Fortunately, CPQ as both a process and a tool eases or even completely eliminates these pain points. By automating manual tasks, connecting all sources of data, and helping your reps sell better and smarter, CPQ not only solves existing problems, but it sets your organization up for future growth as well.

Automate manual tasks

- CPQ streamlines routine, time-consuming tasks involved in the pricing and quoting process.
- CPQ manages risk more effectively than a human team can by automating your pricing structure and ensuring mistakes aren't made.
- CPQ automates the amendment creation process, making add-ons and upsells seamless.
- CPQ frees up sales reps' time by guiding them to the proper product configurations.
- CPQ sets up automatic, on-brand quote templates so you can impress prospects with each quote while still using accurate, up-to-date, contextual info.
- CPQ reduces quote approval time with automated workflows.

Connect all sources of data

- CPQ is channel-agnostic, which means it unifies all sales channels under one platform—a single source of truth.
- CPQ connects all pricing databases for one reliable system of record.

THE DEFINITIVE QUOTE-TO-CASH GUIDE

- CPQ seamlessly integrates with other CRM and QTC products, making both CPQ and your other tools more powerful together than alone.

- CPQ decreases reporting time by integrating with other data sources and creating dashboards that can be leveraged instantly.

- CPQ eliminates silos by allowing each person with the right permissions in your organization to access the sales information they need.

- CPQ reduces the amount of pricing and configuration errors by leveraging all current, relevant data sources.

Help reps sell better and smarter

- CPQ's dynamic pricing feature is fueled by an AI engine that monitors sales intel in real time.

- CPQ creates guided-selling strategies.

- CPQ allows for smart business rules to govern approvals, prices, discounts, and more.

- CPQ generates more renewal opportunities by using previous pricing logic configured in CPQ.

- CPQ benefits the bottom line by presenting accurate information in a timely way, empowering reps to sell more to both new and repeat customers with easy-to-access data.

- CPQ decreases time from quote to close.

- CPQ makes your sales team more productive.

- CPQ increases product and pricing visibility throughout the entire organization.

- CPQ helps decrease average discount levels and improve margins and the bottom line.

- CPQ gives you the opportunity to enable self-service ordering for your partners and customers, reducing the administrative burden on your own teams.

Benefits You Can Expect

The following are examples of metrics as measured and reported by companies after going live on their CPQ implementation:

- 28 percent reduction in sales cycle time[4]
- 49 percent higher proposal volume per rep per month[5]
- 105 percent greater average deal size[6]
- 33 percent faster quote generation[7]
- 25 percent increase in productivity[8]
- 38 percent reduction in quote pricing errors[9]
- 15 percent increased efficiency[10]
- 27 percent increase in sales revenues[11]
- 32 percent increase in lead conversion[12]
- 34 percent increase in customer satisfaction[13]
- 56 percent faster deployment[14]

Place in the Quote-to-Cash Journey

As we've touched on a few times now, automation is the key to tying the entire CPQ process together. With an automated CPQ system configuring your products and services, consistently pricing according to your selected models, and generating and tracking approved quotes, your return on investment is enormous.

Make no mistake about it: your success criteria for your CPQ project will not be met without automation. Not only are you saving your sales reps time by making them more productive, but you're also empowering them. The materials in their hands are better and more accurate than those generated manually. They can finally stop worrying about administrative tasks and focus on what they do best: sell.

CPQ is the first step into a full quote-to-cash process: it allows you to put together products and services and their associated pricing as a technically and commercially viable solution in front of your end customers.

In the next chapter, we will look at an often overlooked but important component of QTC: Contract Lifecycle Management or CLM.

CHAPTER TWO

CLM

Dyno Nobel is a giant in the global commercial explosives industry. Its workforce of over 3,770 men and women includes some of the industry's most highly trained blasters, spread across 32 manufacturing facilities on three continents, producing over 54 million pounds of packaged explosives and more than 1.2 million tons of ammonium nitrate.

With their increase in size and capacity for output, and without an automated contract lifecycle management system, Dyno Nobel was struggling. The company's contracting process was manual and time-consuming, and contracts were stored in disparate drives and folders. With limited ability to track use and changes to approved forms, Dyno Nobel regularly dealt with inefficient contract turnaround.

(According to Forrester, it takes an average of 3.4 weeks to create and approve a contract.[1]) If the company was serious about continuing to scale, something would have to change.

What would you do in Dyno Nobel's situation?

Fortunately, there is a solution, and it fits perfectly with CPQ. To meet their goals, Dyno Nobel reached out to Simplus for help with implementing a contract lifecycle management (CLM) system. In doing so, Dyno Nobel reduced customer onboarding time by 50 percent, saved over 30 hours per month, and increased the number of accounts their staff could handle by five to seven times.[2]

These results are not unique to Dyno Nobel; they are achievable by anyone effectively using a CLM system. In this chapter, we'll go over what CLM is, the pain points that a CLM system addresses, how it does so, the major players in the ecosystem, and its place in the overall QTC journey.

WHY YOU NEED CLM

01 DOCUMENT STANDARDIZATION
Generated documents in a standard format

02 VERSION CONTROL & DOCUMENT CHANGES
Document changes tracked and managed

03 DOCUMENT SEARCH & REPORTING
Central repository for searching and reporting on documents

04 DOCUMENT APPROVALS & SIGNATURE
Streamlined and automated approval processes and signatures

05 REDUCED TIME-TO-CONTRACT SIGNATURE
Increased win rate

CLM 6 BEST PRACTICES

01 PREPARE YOUR DOCUMENTS
Organize existing documents, standardize document templates

02 DEFINE YOUR PROCESSES
What? Who? Why? How?

03 PREPARE SALESFORCE
Configuration of Accounts, Opportunities, and other custom objects

04 PREPARE CPQ
Configuration of Quote, Product, & Pricing data

05 PREPARE YOUR TEAM
Listen to concerns and obtain buy-in

06 DEFINE PRIORITIES & KEY OBJECTIVES
Crawl, walk, and then run!

Definition of CLM

Gartner defines CLM as

> a solution and process for managing the life cycle of contracts
> created and/or administered by or impacting the company. These
> include third-party contracts, such as outsourcing, procurement,
> sales, nondisclosure, intellectual property, leasing, facilities
> management and other licensing, and agreements containing
> contractual obligations now and in the future.[2]

Aberdeen reports that contract approval time drops an average of 82 percent when using a CLM solution.[3]

Contract Management Pain Points

An effective CLM system makes life easier for both the seller and the buyer. Let's take a look at what each party is looking for and the respective challenges they have to overcome.

Seller

For the modern seller, efficiency is top of mind: He is constantly looking for ways to improve the time to signature/value. He wants to increase the efficiency of closing deals to quickly provide valuable solutions to his clients so he can stay ahead of the competition. In order to achieve that vision, though, the process from generating a contract through to its signature or execution must be streamlined and efficient. Without a CLM system, the modern seller faces the following challenges:

- There is no single, central, electronic location to manage contracts. Contracts are stored and managed in multiple disparate systems, resulting in a lack of a single source of truth for contracts.

- The manual creation of contracts results in increased time to contract generation and risk for human error.
- Contract approvals, redlines, negotiations, and signature are managed manually and via email, slowing the contract process and making contract changes and version control time-consuming and cumbersome to access.
- There is no visibility into the contract stage or status, making it nearly impossible to keep the ball rolling in terms of next steps.
- Lack of approval automation slows the contract process and incurs a heavy burden on legal teams.

For the seller to be satisfied, he will need a system that can do the following:

- Provide a single, central, electronic location to create and maintain contracts in order to provide a single source of truth into contracts.
- Automate contract approvals, redlines, and negotiation processes to speed up contract processes, increase time to value, and reduce the burden on legal teams.
- Create a self-service model for sales teams and reduce risks associated with manual contract generation by standardizing the creation of contracts.
- Create contract reports and analytics to identify contract status and stage and reduce bottlenecks.

Buyer

The modern buyer wants access to the contract without being bogged down its upkeep. She needs visibility into contract total spend and, like the seller, wants contracts and contract data to be easily searchable. She wants to spend less time on managing contract processes and more time managing operational efficiencies. However, without a CLM system, the modern buyer faces the following challenges:

- There is no single, central, electronic location in which to manage contracts. Contracts are stored and managed in multiple disparate systems, resulting in a lack of a single source of truth for contracts.

- Contract approvals, redlines, negotiations, and signature are managed manually and via email, slowing the contract process and making contract changes and version control time-consuming and cumbersome to access.

- Key contract information such as vendor spend, commitments, warranties, and obligations are time-consuming and nearly impossible to search for.

- There is no visibility into the contract stage or status, making it nearly impossible to keep the ball rolling in terms of next steps.

- Lack of approval automation slows the contract process and incurs a heavy burden on legal and finance teams.

For the buyer to be satisfied, she will need a system that can do the following:

- Provide a single, central, electronic location for creating and managing contracts in order to provide a single source of truth into contracts

- Automate contract approvals, redlines, and negotiations to speed up contract processes and reduce the burden on finance and legal teams

- Associate metadata to contracts to provide quick access and visibility into key contract information

- Create contract reports and analytics to identify contract status and stage and reduce bottlenecks

How a CLM System Can Help

A CLM system answers the needs of the seller and buyer alike. Let's highlight some of the key capabilities of a CLM system and how they can help.

Contract Repository

A single, central, electronic contract repository provides a single source of truth for searching and accessing contracts, providing the following capabilities:

- Contract organization into folders
- Metadata tagging of contracts to allow for easily searching and accessing contracts
- Contract security to open up and control access to different parties
- Contract version control

Contract Analytics

Contract analytic capabilities provide a method to easily search for, retrieve, and report on key contract data by offering the following capabilities:

- Metadata tagging of contracts, allowing for easy searching and reporting on key contract information.
- Create reports to highlight operational inefficiencies and status of in-process contracts.

Document Generation

Document generation capabilities provide a way to standardize the contract generation process by offering the following capabilities:

- Automatic generation of contracts from a standard template prepopulated with key information such as account, product, and pricing information, reducing the need for a contract request process by providing a self-service model for sales reps
- Dynamic content within templates, reducing the need for maintaining multiple template versions by condensing them down to a smaller amount

Workflow Automation

Most CLM systems offer a robust workflow engine, providing a way to speed up the contract process and increase efficiency by offering the following capabilities:

- Automatic routing of contract approvals to necessary parties, reducing email clutter and manual labor associated with approval assignments
- A redlining process automatically managed via the workflow so that external party changes can be easily identified and reviewed
- Automatic notifications to easily notify stakeholders of key contract events and provide follow-up notifications to keep the contract process moving

Clause Library

A digital clause library reduces the burden on the legal team by offering nonstandard term access to sales and by providing insight into frequently requested term changes by offering the following capabilities:

- Core location in which standard and nonstandard terms can be managed and easily modified
- Allows users to easily access and populate nonstandard terms within contracts without requiring legal input
- Automatic tracking of frequently requested changes to standard terms

Electronic Signature

Electronic signature capabilities reduce the need to prepare, route, and sign contracts manually by offering the following capabilities:

- Digital tagging of signature blocks in contracts
- Automatic routing of contract signing to signers and cosigners, reducing the time associated with manually routing for signature and providing an audit trail into who's signed the contract and when
- Digital signing process, easily storing and tracking signatures applied to the contract

Artificial Intelligence

Artificial intelligence capabilities within a CLM tool can provide numerous benefits to easily search for and analyze contract-related metadata by providing the following capabilities:

- Automatic OCR of contracts to extract metadata from an uploaded file
- Automatic metadata tagging to uploaded contracts

- Advanced analysis on key contract data such as risks, obligations, and commitments

Integrations

APIs within a CLM system can be leveraged to seamlessly receive and send data to and from external systems to keep data in sync from contracts across other external applications. Some use cases for leveraging integrations to/from your CLM system include the following:

- Retrieve information from a CRM tool such as Salesforce or Oracle SAP to automatically populate Vendor and client information into contracts.

- After contract execution, send key contract data such as payment/billing terms, commitments, and obligations to an external billing, invoicing, or ERP system to ensure the latest information is updated in these systems in close to real time.

HOW CAN CLM HELP?

CONTRACT REPOSITORY

A Single, searchable central repository can help solve compliance issues

- Contract organization into folders
- All documents stored in a single, searchable repository
- Reporting & searching on contracts

CONTRACT ANALYTICS

- Metadata tagging of contracts allows for easy searching and reporting
- Create reports to highlight operational inefficiencies and status of in process contracts

CONTRACT STANDARDIZATION

Standardizing the contract generation process increases speed of contract generation and reduces the risk of manual error

- Improved accuracy in contracts
- Increased speed of contract generation

WORKFLOW AUTOMATION

Leveraging workflows to automate current manual processes can increase the speed of transactions and provide visibility into the contract process

- Approval automation
- Status updates
- Increased speed of deal closure
- Reduction in manual processes

RED-LINING & E-SIGNATURE

Client & partner centric functions can improve the overall client & partner experience and allow for easy reporting and access to transactions

- Reduces the need for manual signing and red-lining
- Allows for visibility into red line changes
- Increased speed of deal closure
- Increased time to revenue recognition

The Industry's Major Key Players

When it comes time to implement CLM for your company, you want to be sure to partner with experts with proven results. Luckily, Simplus is partnered with two of the key players in the ecosystem: Conga and DocuSign SpringCM. Both offer leading solutions for contract lifecycle management and streamlining this part of the QTC process.

Conga

Conga is a proud Salesforce Platinum Partner with over 10 years of experience removing pain points in customers' processes. With over 8,000 passionate customers and 150,000 users worldwide, the platform has been awarded five stars on Salesforce AppExchange, and its app Conga Composer is the No. 1 paid app on AppExchange.

Conga offers a suite of products to assist with streamlining your contract lifecycle management processes, both on and off of the Salesforce platform:

- Conga Composer, Conga's flagstone product, is a document generation solution that integrates tightly with Salesforce to allow for quick and easy generation of contracts from a standardized template prepopulated with Salesforce and CPQ metadata such as account, contact, quote, and quote line item information.

- Conga Orchestrate is a robust rules engine and flow manager with integrated Composer document generation. Declaratively define criteria that will automatically add the correct clauses to your document—based on record types and Salesforce fields—and declaratively define when this process runs to generate your documents automatically. For example, you can utilize product family values, product names, or product types to include specific clauses conditionally. Use the state of the customer's address to automate the inclusion of state governing laws. Use specific options checked on an opportunity or quote to include special provisions, and automate those for approvals—all from within Orchestrate!

- Conga's True Up™ product eliminates the overhead of manually updating the clause library and Salesforce records from requested redline changes, empowering the user to update fields straight from redlines automatically.

- Conga Contracts for Salesforce works hand in hand with Conga Composer to allow for automation of Composer-generated contracts through approvals, redlines, negotiations, and electronic signature, all on top of the Salesforce platform.

- Conga Contracts is an off-platform (not Salesforce native) CLM system that provides a central, core repository for managing and storing contracts in addition to automation capabilities. The Java-based solution offers a relational database which is ideal for managing buy-side contracts and their related metadata such as vendors and other parties.

DocuSign Agreement Cloud

DocuSign announced its release of the Agreement Cloud in early 2019. With a world-class electronic signature and API at its core, DocuSign sought out to create a platform designed to modernize the system of agreement by providing robust capabilities to support multiple different verticals and the most complex of use cases through the four stages of preparing, signing, acting on, and managing agreements:

Prepare

- DocGen for Salesforce allows for quick and easy generation of polished sales contracts directly from Salesforce.
- Guided forms by Intelledox allows for the replacement of complex forms with an intuitive, wizard-style experience.

Sign

- DocuSign's electronic signature functionality provides best-in-class electronic signature capability, which offers support for 43 languages, high security to meet global security standards, compliance with regulation standards such as the US ESIGN Act, sign-from-anywhere capabilities, and more.

Act

- SpringCM offers a best-in-class contract workflow engine, which helps to automate contract approval routing, redline automation, contract notifications, and more.

Manage

- SpringCM's contract repository provides a single, central, electronic location where contracts can easily be searched for, accessed, and managed.
- Total Search by Seal software allows for indexing and searching of agreements, whether inside or outside of DocuSign.
- Intelligent Insights by Seal software offers AI-driven concept searching, clause identification, analytics, and more.

Integrate

- DocuSign's Agreement cloud platform offers over 350 prebuilt integrations, including Salesforce, Google G Suite, SAP Ariba, Microsoft Dynamics, and more.
- APIs and SDKs allow for extending DocuSign eSignature, SpringCM, and other DocuSign products.

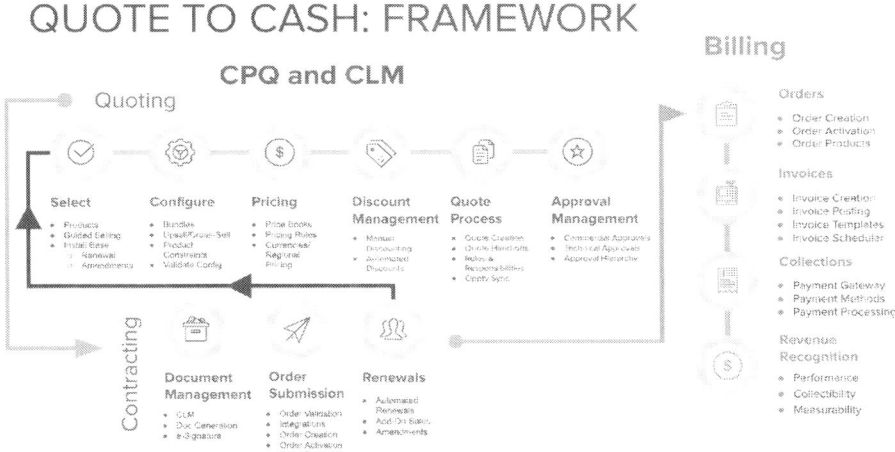

QUOTE TO CASH: FRAMEWORK

CLM's Place in the Quote-to-Cash Journey

As we continue this book, keep in mind that we are not discussing optional paths you can take to improve your business operations. These chapters aren't isolated aspects of doing business so much as they are interconnected steps of a continuous path that is QTC. To ensure their connection, you must approach these principles with a mind geared toward integration. Integration is vital to ensuring high productivity, increased efficiency, and a satisfying ROI. In this case, integration will include melding CPQ and CLM systems. In SpringCM's 2017 State of Contract Management Report, 70 percent of respondents reported that they had already integrated these solutions.[5]

When it comes time to integrate CPQ and CLM, it is important that you make use of certain best practices. The following tips will help you strike a balance between your solutions and ensure they are both meeting their full potential and empowering one another at the same time.

Manage Products, Pricing, and Discount Approvals in CPQ

Any approvals and negotiations related to products, pricing, or discounting should be managed before the document is generated in CLM. Doing so will allow you to retain a single source of truth for your product, pricing, and discount data within CPQ. CLM applications are not wired to host this type of data. Managing these types of approvals in CLM could result in potentially out-of-sync data between the CPQ and CLM systems.

Leverage CLM for Contract Generation

When it comes to product, pricing, and discount approvals, CPQ should be your go-to system. You'll be using it to approve pricing and products and to handle any approvals that require people to review and sign off on discounts or special product circumstances. In most cases, these approvals will all be taken care of long before any document is generated for your client. While CPQ systems offer document generation capabilities, they are usually limited in their functionality. For example, some data within certain objects can be difficult or impossible to query; the editing of a document after it's been generated can also be a challenge. Document generation is a core feature of most CLM tools, so getting it right is usually key.

Aside from the limitations that a CPQ's document generation tool may have, generating the contract from CPQ can result in having more than one source of truth for your contracts, which can provide challenges when trying to access and search for contracts and related metadata.

Just think about it: were you to generate the document from within CPQ, you would have a much harder time managing a repository for all of your contracts. Generating a document with CLM, however, allows you to begin a central repository for future reporting, tracking, and management of your clause library.

That being the case, you should use a CLM solution for all document generation. It will assume that pricing approvals have already been completed and allow you to easily modify your document templates. Further, leveraging CLM for document generation will make it much easier for you to negotiate terms with a client.

For example, let's look at the statement of work, which includes product and pricing data within it. It will be much easier to revise and fine-tune the price sheet output in CPQ, where it can be collaborated on by both parties, making the approval process much smoother. Once approved, the deal can move on to CLM for contract generation. Instead of juggling multiple versions of the same document over the course of the negotiation, you'll have version control over the multiple iterations of a single contract.

Manage Legal and Term-Related Approvals in CLM

While we recommend that product, pricing, and discount approvals be managed within CPQ, a CLM system also offers robust workflow and automation capabilities. As a core function of most CLM tools, workflows can help to automate the end-to-end contract process after the document has been generated.

Any term-related approvals, such as nonstandard terms, should be managed within your CLM system. CLM workflow capabilities, such as SpringCM's advanced workflow, can automatically route these types of requests to the legal team or whomever else, either before the contract gets generated or after its been reviewed and redlined by the external party.

Clause libraries should be leveraged as your single source of truth for contract terms. Features such as Conga's True Up™ capability allow any requested changes to terms to be automatically synced back to your clause library.

CPQ and CLM

Let's take a look at how CPQ works on it own, alone, versus when it's coupled with a robust CLM tool:

CPQ without CLM

The process outlined in chapter 1 goes on without change. However, you may notice some pain points:

- A more limited clause library
- Limited contract generation capabilities
- No automatic negotiation of the structured data (e.g., the number of days for payment can't be changed easily with CPQ alone)
- Nonexistent redlining capabilities
- Basic set of structured data related to contract negotiation
- Lack of contract version control
- Lack of visibility and reporting on contract status, stage, and duration

CPQ with CLM

- Built-in, automatic redlining capabilities out of the box

- Extensive clause library, including clause terms, allowing for a central repository
- Automated process for contracts, from generating all the way through execution
- Useful, extensive info from contracts (sign date, etc.), managed in a way that is easy to leverage later for renewals
- Advanced electronic signature capabilities
- Dynamic approvals
- Some documents need to go through extensive internal approvals with legal or finance to review terms, differentiate between legal regions, and track the end-to-end status
- A dynamic playbook for the future: the legal team can see what clauses are being negotiated most often with a whole history of contract lifecycle management at the ready
- Automatic conversion of negotiated items back into structured data

Your QTC process is made stronger, more robust, and easier to adopt when CPQ is coupled with CLM. In the next chapter, we will look at the final major component of the Quote-to-Cash process: billing.

CHAPTER THREE

BILLING

To the uninitiated, billing can seem like a mountain of work and a veritable business nightmare. There are orders to satisfy, invoices and bills to fill out, receipts to issue, and payment schedules to arrange and follow. Would that you could simply skip over it, but without this long, tedious process, you'd have no way of organizing and collecting your money, the precious, life-giving blood of your organization.

Think of billing as your business's circulatory system. The blood must flow, or else the whole system will shut down. But your circulatory system doesn't require that you consciously direct its movements: it's automated by your brain to function on its own, side by side with your muscles and organs. In the same way, a good billing system is one that is effortlessly aligned with sales and automated with a dynamic system customized to your business needs.

Fortunately, Salesforce Billing does all this and more. In this chapter, we'll discuss what this service is, why you need it, and how you can get the most use out of it.

PROFITABLE GROWTH – CONTROLLING THE CASH

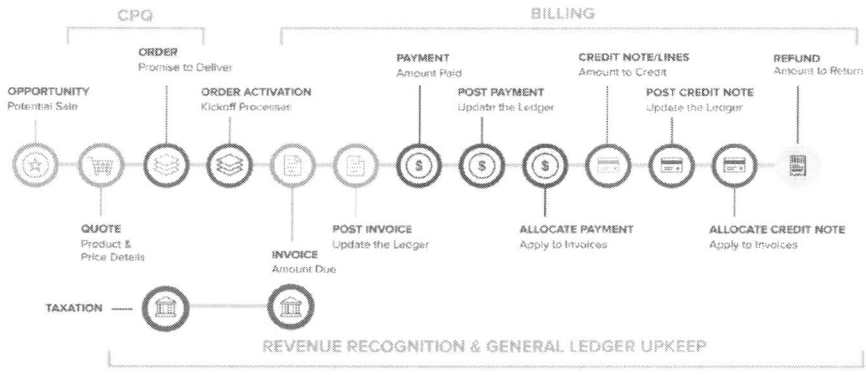

Definitions and Overview

Though it can seem intimidating, billing can easily be simplified into six main areas.

The Order

Salesforce Billing picks up right where CPQ leaves off: the quote. The moment a client accepts a quote, an order can be created.

An order on Salesforce Billing is similar to any checkout process you've encountered on any website. Think to your last purchase: before completing the purchase, you're presented with a list of your intended purchases along with their associated prices, quantities, etc. And that's exactly what an order is: an overview of the products or services being bought along with any relevant details. Salesforce Billing will include dates of order, due dates, and more for each line item, as well as the address with which the order is associated. Further, it will include any relevant preconfigurations or bundles associated therewith according to your CPQ system.

The order itself presents an opportunity to support additional business processes, such as provisioning or service activation. In addition, not every transaction will warrant an immediate charge for every product. The flexibility of the Salesforce Billing platform lets you decide how and when to trigger additional business processes, including how to recognize revenue on a product-by-product basis.

The Invoice

From the client's perspective, the invoice is the bill: it is a rundown of the products and services bought, along with their individual prices and totaled cost. It's what they owe. Salesforce Billing automates the process by considering all of the orders in a given time frame and collecting them into a single invoice, then delivering that invoice to the client. However, you still have control and can determine the time frame and regularity of invoices, be it monthly, quarterly, annually, or some other special arrangement. Besides that, the process is automated, so you never have to worry about keeping track of what you are owed.

- **Usage-Based Pricing**: Under usage-based pricing, you can prepare quotes, contracts, and orders according to the specific goods and services your customers consume. You don't need to worry about searching multiple systems to fill out the paperwork, as the system automatically updates the customer's account with all usage information, renewals, order changes, etc.

- **Evergreen Subscriptions:** For long-term customers, contract renewals are nothing but a disruptive formality. That is, unless you allow for automatic contract renewals. The new system will automatically update quotes, customer opportunities, payments, and revenue reports at set intervals, allowing you to prepare and deliver accurate revenue reports on time and complete orders faster than before.

- **Flexible Invoicing.** The system will automatically bill your customers once they've met specific intervals/milestones you've set. That means you can invoice as soon as a you've delivered a good or service, or you can bill periodically throughout a project's run. Essentially, you can use whatever system works best for you and your clients.

Dunning

Finance teams need the ability not only to report on accounts that are past due and the varying accounts receivable (AR) balances, but they also require the tools necessary to resolve these issues on a case-by-case basis. The dunning process within Salesforce can be built to suit using the flexibility of the platform. Using Salesforce custom reports and workflow allows for the support of dunning and collections processes that meet the needs of your business, either through the UI or through other processes. In addition, Salesforce provides the ability to plug into those solutions built on the platform for systematic notifications to the customer.

Payment Collection

Salesforce Billing has the ability to collect and apply payments for customers either manually or in an automated fashion. There are native integrations with some payment providers allowing your business to streamline the payments process and receive automatic payments for customers. With the use of Advanced AR built within Salesforce Billing, Salesforce Billing can support the application of invoice line level payments to ensure that payments are applied where they are needed most.

AR Management

Accounts receivable reporting and management is available as a standard function in Salesforce Billing. Reporting can be done via dashboards or reports.

Salesforce Billing provides the functionality to customize a general ledger specific to your organization, allowing data such as accounts receivables to flow into your financial management system of choice. This synchronization is critical for managing and reporting on current customer balances as well as managing those accounts that are past due for collections.

Salesforce Billing handles both credits and debits for those scenarios when service credits, sales credits, refunds, returns, or general balances need to be adjusted. These types of adjustments are seamless across both CPQ and Billing and allow for full transparency to the current customer's account status. This can be an effective weapon for ensuring your customers remain happy and satisfied with your products and services.

GL Transactions

Salesforce Billing allows for the customization of a revenue finance book, finance periods, and specific billing treatment rules allowing for pointed transactional data to the correct GL accounts, including credit and debit entries for specific products and scenarios. In addition, this gives power to recognizing revenue across multiple legal entities.

Order products can be consolidated or organized and pointed to GL rules, which govern what happens when and how the GL is impacted on a transaction basis. Additionally, the relationships between the objects within the platform allow for transparency (lookups) across the platform to validate or review the impact that each transaction has to your GL.

Typical Integration Points

In the subscription economy, a billing system becomes the center of the universe for the enterprise. In order to capture the complete functionality and data, a business typically has to integrate other systems to the platform to get data to the requesting parties.

For usage transaction processing, integrations to a usage collection engine provide the data necessary to rate usage and charge customers for their usage-based services.

General billing tasks can be unique to your business. However, a taxation processor, an invoice and dunning notification (mailer format), and a payment processor can all be integrated directly with the billing system. Many solutions exist, built directly on the Salesforce platform, making integration much easier.

Finally, the information from the billing system may need to get into the financial management system or enterprise resource planning tool (ERP). Salesforce Billing makes the setup, maintenance, and integration seamless to your ERP of choice.

For information collection, processing, and reporting, integrations for a business intelligence solution or data warehouse are common.

For enterprises with multiple integration points, a middleware platform is typically recommended. The Salesforce platform is now equipped with one of the leading and most innovative integrations solutions available: MuleSoft. For more information on middleware tools and best practices, refer to chapter 13.

Pain Points

Whether you are launching your first subscription product or consolidating multiple solutions with different data models to increase speed to market, there are many pain points that Salesforce billing can assist in addressing.

With new products and services, new go-to-market strategies, and continued evolution in markets, your business has been forced to adapt. Over time, the solutions for gaps in the current systems and system functionality can compile, leaving quite a sophisticated architecture that may eventually result in slowed growth or slower response to market demands.

Many symptoms of this rapid growth and adaptation materialize as the following (to name a few):

- Slow or inefficient time to market for new products or services—selling new services quickly without having to make sure that they are available or entered into the billing system.
- The same product represented differently across multiple systems (SKU proliferation)—products and services carrying the same SKU and product structure from quote to order to bill.
- Inability to effectively or systematically adjust pricing models for market/customer demands—adjusted and negotiated prices consistent in the billing system from the quote.

- Overcustomization to meet the needs of a single application or solution, whether it's integration, more code, or workflows—development to ensure the customer, product, and prices are consistent across QTC.

- Invoice accuracy and the manual efforts to validate—consistency in what was quoted and what the customer is billed for.

- Higher customer support call volume—internal issues become customer-facing ones like an inaccurate bill.

Additionally, growth may lead to multiple systems performing the same business functions, which can be exacerbated as growth becomes international or acquisitions become part of the growth strategy. Differences in data models between systems can result in a loss of data integrity, increased customization, increased technical debt, and increased manual processes (needed to verify/audit/validate).

How Billing Helps

The move to a single platform such as Salesforce enables a consolidated and sophisticated approach to address all of these areas.

Salesforce Billing allows for a seamless integration to CPQ for a single, central source of record for your products and services. New products can be built quickly and launched effectively as they are visible to your sales teams and available from QTC instantaneously. The flexibility of the platform allows for only those customizations that enable your business and not slow growth or acceleration to market dominance.

Salesforce Billing can be integrated into solutions already built on the Salesforce platform to create, customize, and deliver invoices that meet your business requirements and those of your customers. The data required for your invoice is consolidated, lowering the risk of errors and streamlining the process of invoice creation and delivery.

Why You Should Care

Maybe you think that your business is already doing well enough when it comes to billing. After all, you provide your goods and/or services, and your customers pay. Simple, right?

What you may not see, however, is all of the errors that are keeping your profits down or the missed opportunities that could have driven them up. In an ideal world, you want a full, 360-degree view of your customers to know what's going well and where you can improve. That's only possible if you're able to keep your billing information visible and side by side with your sales and service data. Let's take some time to review the many benefits that come from a billing system.

Reduce Manual Work

Connecting with a billing system is a perfect way to save your teams the tedious and repetitive manual work that takes little to no skill but hours of valuable time. By automating certain tasks, you can immediately free up your teams to focus on tasks more worthy of their qualifications and attention. This includes your sales teams, customer support teams, and your finance teams. Sales can have the automated reports necessary to drive upsell and cross-sell opportunities in a manner that speeds up the lead-to-contract or lead-to-order process and assists them in providing the right products and services that customers are looking for at the right time.

Customer support teams are able to provide the level of support necessary on the first contact in the least amount of interfaces to provide expedient and efficient service that results in happy customers—no more searching across a multitude of systems to learn about the customer.

Finance is able to cut down on those processes that result from manual "fixes" in the upstream systems: creative processes that may support one system, process, or team, but result in a lengthy month-end close process and higher risk in financial reporting errors.

Generate Error-Free Bills

With automation comes a natural drop in costly human error. But it's more than the system doing the work for your employees: the system enables your employees to do their other tasks more efficiently. With a billing system, salespeople are guided step by step through the process of preparing quotes and generating orders, ensuring that no factors are forgotten or overlooked. Gone are the days in which a salesperson could send off a flawed document for the finance or customer service team to take responsibility for. Billing is the natural continuity to your CPQ process, and a seamlessly integrated solution guarantees an error-free flow of data into your billing system.

View Customer Purchase and Payment History

Off the top of your head, can you say when a customer last purchased a software upgrade? Do you know how often another regular customer buys a specific product? Or do you know which customers are under warranty and which are about to expire? Having all of this information laid out in front of you as a purchase history empowers your sales and service teams alike, informing them of your customers' needs even before your customers are aware of them themselves.

At the same time, do you know exactly when your clients are paying their bills? Do you know how often payment comes past due and why they're late? One study found that 47 percent of businesses admit to paying their suppliers after their agreed-upon date.[1] Maybe these tardy customers are dissatisfied with their service or else skeptical of the invoice, leading them to drag their feet. Left unaddressed, these concerns can ultimately drive your clients away. With a simple view of your clients' payment history, you can easily flag and investigate possible problems before they cost you customer loyalty or else drop customers that are more trouble than they're worth.

See Volume Purchases

Many organizations err in not making their volume purchases readily visible to their sales teams. The problem is that while the sales team is responsible for structuring the original deal, an order management team takes over processing the deal. However, if the sales team can see the details of volume purchases, they can offer their customers better pricing packages based on their activity (e.g., restructuring a deal or offering a volume discount). Salesforce Billing enables you to do just that with usage-based billing.

Simplify Billing

Perhaps you think your current ERP (enterprise resource planning) is enough to see you through billing. Unfortunately, most traditional ERPs only account for orders and revenue associated with single transactions. If you're dealing with usage/subscription-based products or services, and your subscription pricing intentionally changes over time (e.g., via price ramps), you'll need Salesforce Billing to simplify your processes. After all, you'll need to account for one special circumstance after another: renewals, upgrades, prorations, add-ons, trial periods, one-time setup fees, and so forth. Salesforce Billing is designed specifically to manage all of these complex billing requirements, saving you from hassles and headaches.

Offer Flexible Billing Arrangements

No matter how set in stone you think your pricing model is, you'll find that just about every customer is an exception to the rule. While some may be willing to pay according to your timeline, more will want to set their own schedule, paying on specific dates or at regular intervals. And when customers don't pay on time, you may need to apply late fees.

No matter what exceptions you may encounter, Salesforce Billing offers the flexibility you need to meet your customers' needs. And with all of the many payment processing apps available through the AppExchange, you have unprecedented ability to meet the needs and preferences of your customers with flexible billing arrangements.

Strengthen Customer Relationships

Traditionally, ERP systems have prioritized the management of ordering and billing processes. However, the raw data produced in these processes does little to help anyone outside of the finance team to build relationships with customers. Salesforce Billing takes this into consideration and automatically links customers' billing records to their Salesforce profiles. Salespeople and customer service teams can easily access these profiles and use them to build a 360-degree customer view. Salesforce then continues to mine data on customers to generate actionable business insights, further enabling you to build strong relationships. You're also able to use Salesforce to build a self-service portal for your customers, allowing them to resolve bill-related issues on their own.

Leverage Usage and Subscription-Based Billing

With subscription- and usage-based products, billing quickly becomes even more critical for your organization. A single platform from QTC allows for faster modifications to your customers' subscriptions and a clear view of how your customers are using the products and services they pay a subscription for. This transparency enables your sales, support, and finance teams throughout the customer journey and provides them with the data they need to elegantly guide a customer to those products and services the customer will find the most useful for their needs. This increases customer satisfaction and reinforces the benefits of the long-term relationship that comes from providing subscription services.

How to Use Billing

Now that we've established the what and the why, let's take some time to establish the how. In particular, we'll go over how to get your Salesforce Billing set up and integrated with CPQ, and then discuss best practices.

How to Integrate Billing with CPQ

Integrating billing with CPQ isn't as difficult as you may think it is. Salesforce Billing offers resources for integration that, while not enabled by default, are still free and well worth your investigation. For example, Salesforce Billing offers tax integration and payment gateway services.

Salesforce offers extensive guides and resources to help with integration, as well as a whole network of consulting partners who are experts at doing just that. But to start, here are some things to keep in mind when integrating billing with CPQ:

- **Align proration settings:** Since CPQ and billing having independent proration settings, it's important to make sure you first align those settings in each package. This will make sure your organization uses accurate data throughout the QTC process.

- **Integrating can help quote-to-invoice development:** Integrating CPQ and billing is a great way to decrease the time spent on invoices and validation by automating tasks and improving forecasting.

- **Integrating can automate payment deployment:** Billing can connect to countless payment processing vendors, which means your organization can integrate CPQ and billing for a full QTC process that speeds up payment collection and improves cash flow.

- **Additional functionality can still be done with other finance systems:** Integrating billing with CPQ doesn't mean you must abandon the trusted ERP or other backend financial systems. Integrating is simply a way to make sure your organization is sharing information and collaborating between departments for better, faster results all around.

Best Practices for Maximizing Salesforce Billing

As you move forward with your new Salesforce Billing integration, be prepared to put in a good deal of work to really maximize your investment. Here are two tips that will really help your organization hit the ground running.

1. Connect your billing data to the sales platform.

If you want to see real results, you will need to go all-in on your Salesforce investment. Primarily, that will mean doing a thorough review of all your data and connecting all of the relevant data with the sales platform. Doing this will increase everyone's access to data as well as knowledgeable income for the overall sales process. You can still handle part of your billing process in a financial system like ERP—just make sure it's playing nicely with the sales system for maximum benefit. Identifying the connection points between systems is key to this process: for example, some clients use the powerful invoicing engine in Salesforce CPQ and push the resulting invoices directly in the ERP or finance system, where the rest of the process is handled.

2. Get your service team on board.

Salesforce Billing has applications beyond your sales and accounting teams. The visibility offered by Salesforce Billing has a special application for your customer service reps. Leveraging Salesforce Billing and the insights it offers into customer ordering and payment habits can give your reps greater clarity to their cases.

In addition to these two tips, there is plenty of work still ahead of you in getting the most out of a full QTC solution. Part one has introduced the three key tools to QTC: CPQ, CLM and billing. But in the upcoming part two of this book, we'll look at where QTC fits in with the processes of your organization.

PART
TWO

WHERE DOES QUOTE-TO-CASH FIT?

CHAPTER FOUR

SALES CYCLE

Salespeople are on the frontlines of your business, acting on leads, negotiating with prospective clients, and closing deals. They are the soldiers of your QTC process, moving the gears that keep your business going.

In this chapter, we'll look at what to do in your first meeting with a client, how to deal with rejection, and how QTC fits into the sales cycle.

What to Do in a First Meeting

Your first meeting with a potential client sets the tone for the rest of your relationship—as well as determining whether or not there will be a relationship at all. When meeting, here are five practices that, if put into practice, will set your salespeople up for the win.

Define Success

Record-setting basketball coach John Wooden defined success as "peace of mind which is a direct result of self-satisfaction in knowing you did your best to become the best you are capable of becoming."[1] A quick Google search will bring up this answer and hundreds more, some similar, some radically different.

Before you can help a customer succeed, you need to understand how they define and measure success. Does it lie in the number of units sold? Employee buy-in? Growth? Whatever their goal is, gauge how ambitious it is. Are they simply trying to maintain or raise the status quo? Or are they truly trying to reach new heights? Those customers who do the latter are much more likely to take a chance on something new, and that's the kind of customer you want to do business with.

Identify the Decision-Makers

Who a customer sends to speak with you says volumes about their intent to do business. If your first meeting is with a representative, you'll want to win him or her over before you can move on to the real gatekeepers. But if you're meeting with the actual decision-maker—the one with the authority to sign the deal into effect—chances are the decision is already half made.

Of course, this isn't a matter of asking who the decision-makers are point-blank. Exercise subtlety by asking what the approval process will be like, when you can expect to receive an answer, and how you can help them to get through the process. The more receptive they are to your questions, the more likely your success.

Look for Deciding Factors

When you ask what the deciding factors are in the deal, don't accept buzzword answers like "budget" or "timeline." While they may be true, they don't represent the entire truth. (Just think of how often you make financial decisions based on quality or experience rather than price.) For example, Gallup's 2014 State of the American Consumer report found that

> customers only shop based on price when price is the only thing that separates competing offerings. In other words, customers shop based on price when there is no emotional connection to a particular retailer—when they are not engaged.[2]

That being the case, if you can engage your customers, you can overcome their buzzwords. To do this, listen to your customers. Ask questions, clarify, and listen some more. Try to figure out where your offering fits within their larger company goals.

Compare Timelines

The early bird may catch the worm, but sometimes it may not need that worm until late afternoon. In your meeting, be sure to ask when the customer will actually need your goods and services. You may find that you won't be needed for months or even years down the road. These long-term leads can go to the marketing department for nurturing.

On the other hand, you may have a customer who is eager to get started right away—too eager, in fact. They may be demanding a turnaround that is either faster than you can deliver or else will compromise the quality of the end product or service. So be honest about your capabilities. They may be open to adjusting if they realize their request is unreasonable. And if they don't have a timeline at all, you can show them how to build one out.

Compare Offerings with Needs

In any deal, you may find that it's not a matter of convincing the customer that you are the right solution. Sometimes, it's about learning for yourself whether or not you're right. Compare your offerings with their needs. Do you have what they need? Better to learn this early in the negotiation process than later, when both parties have dedicated a significant amount of time to nurture the relationship.

Dealing with "No"

The negotiation process is full of highs and lows. But sometimes you encounter full stops. A price is presented, or a service is offered, and the answer comes back: "No."

While this may seem like an end to the discussion, a "No" can actually be an opportunity to continue. As such, rather than trade pleasantries and beat around the bush in order to avoid rejection, it is wiser to push the discussion to get to that first "No"—because "Yes" is only just around the corner. Let's discuss what actions to take when confronted with a "No" and how to know when it's time to say it yourself.

How to Make the Client Say "No"

The sooner your client says "No," the sooner you can either course-correct or part ways. Use the following tactics to push your clients to the make-or-break point:

1. **Ask as many relevant questions as you can.**

You won't get an answer without first asking a question. But these questions must be relevant to the deal. Ask plenty of discovery questions, especially those with open-ended answers, and listen.

2. **Dig deep.**

As they answer your questions, dig deep into their answers. Discuss them. This will transform your meetings from Q&A sessions into real discussions, which will invite your customers to feel more comfortable sharing their concerns with you; concerns like the following:

"We're a little set in our ways."

"We're not sure we can justify the expense."

"This is too similar to our competitor."

While each of these may seem like a rejection, there's plenty of room to learn more. You're getting a feel for budget constraints, competition, company culture, and other details that will be important for closing the deal. In the right hands, a client's objections can be used to turn a "No" into a "Yes."

3. **Course correct.**

You can usually tell when a customer starts to back off. Even if they don't come right out and say, "That's not what we're looking for," you should still be able to tell from body language or more subtle verbal cues. It could be that they don't entirely trust you yet, they may not understand the question, or it's too early for them to give you confidential information. Don't be discouraged, though. Take the opportunity to adjust your questions and put them at ease.

When You Should Say "No"

There will come times when it is up to you to say "No" to the client. It may not be easy, though. Salespeople are naturally inclined to please others. But there are situations where it is the best course of action for all concerned:

1. When they're asking for more than you can deliver

Many sales reps are willing to go to the moon and back for their customers. They'll do whatever it takes to keep a customer happy, even if doing so is detrimental to the company. This is why it is so important for salespeople to know exactly what is within the company's power and what is not: so that when a customer asks too much, the salesperson knows to say "No." After all, there are some customers who will ask for more every time they get a "Yes."

2. When you know enough

During the course of your discovery questions process, you may come to learn that you and the customer simply aren't a good match. The reasons are endless: they need what you can't provide, their industry is outside of your expertise, their competitor is already a client of yours, etc.

What Salespeople Want from Quote-to-Cash

When you first land a lead, your primary goal is to understand the client and the end solution that they're trying to reach. As it pertains to sales, your goal is to get the most information consistently and with discounts approved through the process as quickly as possible.

As a salesperson, time is money. If you're in a high turnover, you will want to check off as many of the following as quickly as possible.

1. Accuracy

Let's say you're selling widgets, and your salespeople have 20 different widget options to try and sell. However, the options don't stop at 20: there are all sorts of parent and child options that come along with them, and these options need to load automatically and accurately. That's as much for your benefit as the salesperson as it is for your delivery team. The last thing you want is to be able to arrive at two different prices when going through the quote generation process. And if ensuring accuracy requires two weeks spent researching what all goes together and in what combinations, your ability to close deals drops significantly.

2. Internal Insight

Internal insight is the ability to look in the backend and see what is going on in other areas of the business. Is it tied directly to inventory? Is it tied directly to resource availability? Can we estimate start dates based on this?

3. Quick Quotes

Let's say you want to have the ability to send out ROM (rough order of magnitude). When you send to an actual quote, then you want (1) to make sure everything is approved and tightened up and (2) to have the ability to have first-time customer meetings and give them estimates.

4. Pricing Options

All discounts should already be built into the system, eliminating the need for manual calculation and guesswork. This will save you the embarrassment of returning to a customer after closing a deal just to tell them you gave the wrong price.

5. Approvals

If you want to go in and add a discount, that change must be routed correctly for approval, ensuring you get your change approved quickly.

6. Options

Your salespeople would like options when it comes to executing the quote process. For example, they like the choice between a physical print out and a DocuSign document with eSignature capabilities. They may also prefer to be able to email preliminary quotes before the finalized document.

7. Flexibility

While it is important to give your customers pricing options, salespeople benefit from not having to follow those pricing options exactly. They need the flexibility to adjust price offers based on negotiation. When a customer comes back from negotiation with a new offer, a rigid price list is just a brick wall preventing your salespeople from closing the deal.

8. Forecasting

It is important for salespeople as well as for the VP of sales to be able to say—based on the sales process and any outstanding quotes—where exactly the money will fall. For example, the forecast may be used to estimate how many people you need to hire to fulfill that order.

As you can see, CPQ provides significant assistance to salespeople by enabling them to be more productive on one side (automation of the quoting process and logic), but also by helping them understand what their limits are both in terms of product offerings (dependencies and exclusions in the product catalog) and in terms of pricing (discount visibility and transparency against approval authority). This helps them navigate through the "Yes" and "No" responses to the prospects and clients they are negotiating with.

However, when the sale is closed (hopefully with the assistance of CPQ), some downstream processes will trigger. The next chapter will focus on one of them: fulfillment.

CHAPTER FIVE
FULFILLMENT

O nce the deal has been finalized and the ink on the contracts has dried, the fulfillment process begins. Fortunately, this step is the most straightforward of the entire QTC process: all of the conditions have already been laid out and agreed upon by both parties in the contract. However, it is still a process that needs oversight, and a QTC solution is vital to ensuring just that. After all, changes may be made to the order at any time, and you need to make sure that those changes are reflected in the final product. Using a fully integrated system that provides a complete view of the customer, you can do just that. With a full QTC solution, you can be sure that all necessary parties have access to the right information.

From a best-practice perspective, once a quote has been approved and accepted, it should be locked in the system. The fulfillment process often requires data beyond products and prices. Therefore, such data should be collected and stored in a different place than the quote, especially if it was unknown or not available during the quoting cycle. In addition, most ERP systems use a concept of "sales order" or "customer order" to feed the fulfillment process. Therefore, you should carefully consider how the quote information will be translated into order information that can be consumed by your fulfillment process, and using a "staging" object between the quote and the sales order in your ERP system is generally a good practice. If you use Salesforce Billing in addition to Salesforce CPQ, you are required to convert your quotes into orders, as the order object is used by Salesforce Billing to feed the billing process.

Converting Quotes to Orders

Salesforce CPQ offers powerful, out-of-the-box order management functionality, and you should definitely consider taking advantage of it.

First and foremost, decide whether you want a single order per quote or need to split a quote into multiple orders, as allowing multiple orders per quote is driven by a package-level configuration setting. Don't forget to potentially allow negative orders (for downgrade quotes) or even zero-quantity order products; these settings are specified at the Salesforce platform level, independently from the CPQ settings.

One major criterion to decide to split a quote into multiple orders is whether or not you will have staged deliveries of the products and services purchased by your customer. With staged deliveries, shipment dates or subscription start date will be different from what you specified on your quote or quote lines. For example, consider the following scenarios:

- You sold two pieces of equipment, but you can only ship the first one as the other must be manufactured first because it's not in inventory. If you sold a maintenance contract (usually a subscription-based service), the start date of the maintenance will be different for each piece of equipment since they ship at different dates.

- You sold a multiphase project. The second phase will not start before the first is completed. Therefore, you will start by delivering only products and services required for phase one, which could all be on a single order. A few weeks or months later, when you start phase two, you create an order with only products and services associated with phase two.

- You sold products and services going to multiple locations, and your fulfillment process requires a separate order for each ship-to address. Your client might require that you bill them per location as well, and creating a separate order per location might be easier for your billing system.

The above are the most common examples where splitting a quote into multiple orders makes sense and helps with downstream processes, especially fulfillment and billing. Examine carefully how your own fulfillment process is designed and decide accordingly, taking into account all downstream processes.

Another best practice consideration relates to automation. Salesforce CPQ allows you to create orders (including multiple orders per quote), either manually or via automation.

The manual order creation functionality will guarantee that you preserve the bundle structure as needed. This is critical to make sure that future amendments and renewals will work as expected.

When automating the process, Salesforce CPQ allows you to split a quote into multiple orders by quote line group, specified filtering criteria, or both. It is important that you do not break the bundle structure during this process; therefore, design your filtering criteria accordingly.

For each order and order product created, you can specify a start date that is different from the start date specified on the corresponding quote or quote line. When selling subscription-based products and services in the context of a staged delivery, it is important to track the actual start date of such subscriptions not only to control the next renewal anniversary date but also because the actual start date is often the billing start date as well. In such scenarios, your install base (contracts/subscriptions and assets) will be generated from the order data instead of from the quote.

The most common examples of actual/final start dates for subscription-based products and services are the following:

- Delivery date
- Installation date
- Go-live date

Does your company make use of these concepts? If yes, you will greatly benefit from using the order management functionality in CPQ and potentially split your quotes into multiple orders.

CPQ Complexities Impacting Fulfillment

Because CPQ integrates powerful capabilities to support the subscription-based model, amendments and renewals can introduce some complexities for your fulfillment team. These complexities come from how you provision upgrades or downgrades, and terminations or cancellations.

With the rich data model in Salesforce CPQ, you are fortunately just a few calculations away from providing the right data to your downstream systems.

Case of Renewals

In a renewal scenario, the quantity on each quote line represents not only what is renewed, but potentially an associated upgrade (increase in quantity) or downgrade (decrease in quantity). Your fulfillment team might have to process this quantity slightly differently than a new business scenario because they should normally only have to deal with the upgrade or downgrade portion of the renewal quantity. As a result, you might have to compute the fulfillment quantity since it's not provided by Salesforce CPQ as of this writing.

Case of Amendments

An amendment in Salesforce CPQ typically represents an upgrade or downgrade transaction that occurs midcontract. Therefore, Salesforce CPQ calculates all the necessary information in this context and natively provides the quantity increase or decrease that your fulfillment team will have to deal with.

Ramp and Escalator Deals

As a reminder, a ramp deal is a deal in which quantity varies over time, while an escalator deal is one in which the price varies over time. The price variation can be the result of a different level of discount between time segments, or of an uplift (or downlift) from one time segment to the next.

In Salesforce CPQ, ramp deals and escalator deals are best represented using MDQ (multidimensional quoting). This powerful functionality allows the creation of time-based segments for which the user can vary the quantity or the price (via discount or uplift). In the data model, each time segment is represented by a separate quote line.

An escalator deal might have no impact on how you provision your products and services since it's just a representation of a price variation, but a ramp deal will likely have to be handled so that future increases or decreases of quantities can be properly addressed over time as they are supposed to occur based on the contract signed with your end customers.

Subscription Products and Services

If you modify the start date at the order or order-product level, make sure you also modify the end date accordingly to preserve the term of the line item. Changing the term leads to a different proration and therefore a different total price or TCV (total contract value). Salesforce CPQ will not recalculate the prorated prices in the context of the order object; it can only do it on the quote object.

If you need to keep the original end date despite the changed start date, you might need to adjust your business process and go back to modify the quote to guarantee accurate pricing. The change in process might include unlocking the quote, reapproving it, and seeking a new acceptance from your customer, depending on your company policies.

The more you try to automate your fulfillment process, the more attention you will have to pay to the complexities mentioned above so that no error occurs during fulfillment. Luckily, the CPQ data model is rich enough to provide most of the necessary information, and the potential minor gaps can be addressed easily with a fairly small level of effort.

Although this book does not include a chapter dedicated to this topic, commission calculations can present similar issues as fulfillment when it comes to amendments and renewals. For example, a renewal could include an increased quantity compared to the prior contract cycle. Many companies compensate their sales reps differently on net-new revenue vs. renewal revenue. In such a situation, additional calculations should be planned in your design to separate the renewal part and the net-new part of the revenue that a single quote line represents. In some cases, such calculations can be tricky.

CHAPTER SIX

REVENUE
RECOGNITION

At first glance, revenue recognition is simple and exactly what it says on the tin: the recognition of revenue. It is the act of recording sales so that they can be reflected on income statements. However, this invites a closer look. For example, when should revenue be recognized? Who in your company is responsible for recognizing revenue? Is it a task reserved entirely for the accounting department, who will then report it to the company executives?

In this chapter, we'll explore the basics of the revenue recognition principle, how it affects all members of an organization, how it differs from cash collected, different methods in which to recognize revenue, and the role CPQ plays in its execution.

The Basics of the Revenue Recognition Principle

In May 2014, the Financial Accounting Standards Board (FASB) and International Accounting Standards Board (IASB) issued International Financial Reporting Standards (IFRS) 15, an update to their revenue recognition principles. The update came with the primary goal of eliminating inconsistencies and providing a framework for accrual accounting. On January 1, 2018, these standards came into play.

According to IFRS 15, in order to recognize revenue, you must first follow these five steps:

1. Identify the contract(s) with a customer
2. Identify the performance obligations in the contract
3. Determine the transaction price
4. Allocate the transaction price to each performance obligation on the basis of the relative stand-alone selling prices of each distinct good or service promised in the contract
5. Recognize revenue when a performance obligation is satisfied by transferring a promised good or service to a customer (which is when the customer obtains control of that good or service)[1]

Unfortunately, while these steps are simple, and while there was a nearly three-and-a-half-year window to get ready, many companies were woefully unprepared. In 2017, Deloitte estimated that nearly 70 percent of polled companies still weren't sure how they would implement the new standard. A disturbing 55 percent hadn't even "started to assess internal controls from a revenue recognition standpoint."

"As this poll indicates, many companies still have further to go in getting ready for the standard," said Ali Sartipzadeh, managing editor at Bloomberg BNA. And Eric Knachel, senior consultation partner at Deloitte & Touche LLP, added,

> Revenue issues are the most common problem underlying accounting enforcement actions. . . . The clock is ticking, and it is critical that disclosures, internal control considerations, and adequate resources be front and center as companies work to adopt the new standard.[2]

The Engine of Revenue Recognition

It's natural for an employee whose job description doesn't explicitly mention accounting to ignore accounting functions altogether. For example, once a salesperson has successfully got a client to buy or sign, it's common for him or her to check out and move on to the next sale, thinking that the job is done. However, revenue recognition cannot be passed off to another party without a second thought. It affects every single employee of the company, and every employee needs to take an active interest in it.

Think of your company as a steam-powered locomotive, and the revenue as the coal. An engineer (a salesperson) may have been responsible for loading the coal onto the train. However, simply sitting on the train isn't enough: the coal must be shoveled into the firebox, which then heats the boiler, producing the steam that powers the engine. But even then, throwing the coal into the firebox indiscriminately won't work. It must be added to the firebox in a steady, timely rhythm: Go too quickly, and you'll burn through the fuel faster than the engine can handle. Go too slowly, and the boiler won't get hot enough to produce the needed amount of steam. It takes a steady application of coal to keep the engine running at peak performance.

In like manner, your company's revenue needs to be recognized (i.e., fed into the firebox) in an accurate and timely manner. When too much or too little is recognized, it impedes your company's ability to budget accurately for its various departments. One department may work with too little funding, while another may dangerously overspend.

Revenue is also vital for gauging your company's health. It's how analysts are able to make valuations, which are then used to determine stock price, secure investment funding, determine merger and acquisition potential, and more.

In short, while individual employees may think they have nothing to do with revenue recognition, they must realize that they are all riding the same train. So they must do anything they can do to ensure the train arrives at the station safely and on time.

Revenue Recognized vs. Cash Collected

You may have noticed earlier that none of the steps mandated by IFRS 15 deal with the actual receipt of payment. That's because we are dealing with an accrual basis of accounting rather than a cash basis. Basically, a cash basis of accounting insists that revenue is recognized upon receipt of a cash payment. Now, confusing revenue recognized with cash payments is a common but rookie mistake.

Let's illustrate the difference with an example: Your construction company signs a contract with a government agency for a development job. As it's such an important deal, and because you know the agency is dependable, you offer net-60 payment terms. After months of work, the cement has been poured, the walls have been raised, and the building interior has been polished. The building is cleared as being up to code, and the job is officially done. With all of your obligations met, you've met all of the IFRS 15 requirements for revenue recognition, and you may now record the revenue from the project, even though you may not receive payment for a few more weeks.

Maybe you went a different route, though. Upon signing the contract, you receive a cash deposit preempting any actual work. Even though the cash payment is on the books, you have yet to fulfill any of your obligations. Therefore, you shouldn't recognize any revenue. Instead, the cash deposit is a liability, which you will offset with recognized revenue once you have met your obligations.

In order to meet IFRS 15 requirements, you must plan for any revenue you are unable to collect. While some companies are always able to collect 100 percent of their recognized revenues, others struggle continuously to collect. In instances where payment is uncertain, it is the responsibility of the accounts receivable team to note the outstanding balance, then lower the number of accounts receivable on the balance sheet. When you have any reason to believe that no payment will be collected at all, you have to fight the temptation to (erroneously) recognize revenue. Remember this: Money owed isn't money at all.

How to Recognize Revenue

There is no one-size-fits-all method for revenue recognition. As there are so many different ways of providing goods and services, it's only natural for companies to differ in their manner of recognition. For example, a company that works on a subscription basis will need to use a different method than one that fills bulk orders. However, no matter how they work, every company is subject to the same IFRS 15 requirements. Here are the four most common ways to recognize revenue.

1. Sales-Based

Revenue for a sale is recognized from the moment that both parties agree to the terms of the sale. This is typical of retail businesses or any company selling products that have already been produced—once the sale has taken place, no further work is required.

2. Installment

It is often the case that a company will not receive full payment upon completion of a service or delivery of a product. These companies may instead opt to record the revenue in installments as the smaller payments are made.

3. Completed Contract

Many companies work on a contract-by-contract basis. For example, think of a software company dealing in short-term implementations. That company would recognize revenue upon completion of the implementation project.

4. Percentage of Completion

Some projects cannot be completed in a short amount of time, and so paying all at once upon completion isn't practical. Instead, the contract may identify regular intervals at which payment will be made. Using a formula, you may estimate the amount of revenue that has been earned during a period by calculating the percentage of the work completed and the expenses incurred in getting to that point.

However you choose to recognize revenue, be sure that you are following the standards set forth by IFRS 15. You'll find that those requirements still leave wiggle room for you to find a method that works best for you, your business, and your customers.

The Importance of CPQ to Revenue Recognition

At this point in the reading, you may believe that your company is already on track. You're abiding by IFRS 15 and recognizing revenue without outside assistance. However, we find that even the most capable clients run into two different problems in executing revenue recognition:

1. **The process is time-consuming.** No matter which method you choose for revenue recognition, it will require careful attention and time spent going over and preparing reports.

2. **The process is filled with errors.** No matter how careful you are, to err is human. Now, while many mistakes may be inconsequential (a misspelling here, a date error there), the wrong digit in the wrong place can be disastrous—or at the very least cost you even more time spent correcting the error. While some companies have built-in systems of checks and balances, many use complex, manual processes that require the finance team to order in food and work late. And that's not even mentioning the fact that the data you're using is often flawed and full of gaps, which trips you up or slows you down.

A CPQ solution could help resolve these issues for you in the following ways:

1. Eliminate the data gaps you would otherwise have to close yourself. If you don't have to close data gaps, you don't have to spend a lot of time painting that picture.

2. Make sure that each data set is complete, correct, and recorded in a consistent way. Many pieces of data are used to feed a decision, so any mistake, however small, must be caught.

3. Make the right data available to accounting for them to then apply the revenue recognition methods. The details from CPQ will come in, allowing your team to hit the ground running.

As you've probably picked up, what a CPQ solution adds to your process is automation. Automation leads to increased ROI. Increased ROI leads to growth. Growth leads to volume. These concepts become more and more important in a subscription-based economy, and even more so with usage-based products and services, as the number of transactions and data points tends to increase exponentially in such contexts.

CPQ makes extensive use of structured data throughout the entire sales process and contract life cycle. This structured data can be used to facilitate revenue recognition calculations not only by providing detailed reporting capabilities but also by creating automation opportunities. But it starts with a sound product catalog structure. You not only need to be able to recognize revenue for each product in your catalog, but you also need to have the proper products in your catalog in order to recognize revenue correctly, based on the performance obligations you define as a company in the context of IFRS 15.

For these reasons, your finance team should be tightly involved from the ground up in your CPQ implementation project, so that their needs in terms of revenue recognition can be incorporated into the structured data consumed or generated by CPQ. This in turn will have a potential impact on how you structure your product catalog, how you implement pricing, and how you present the information to your end customers. This last point is actually critical since terms and conditions included in the quote document submitted for acceptance can have dramatic consequences on how you should recognize revenue.

PART THREE

BEST PRACTICES FOR YOUR QUOTE-TO-CASH JOURNEY

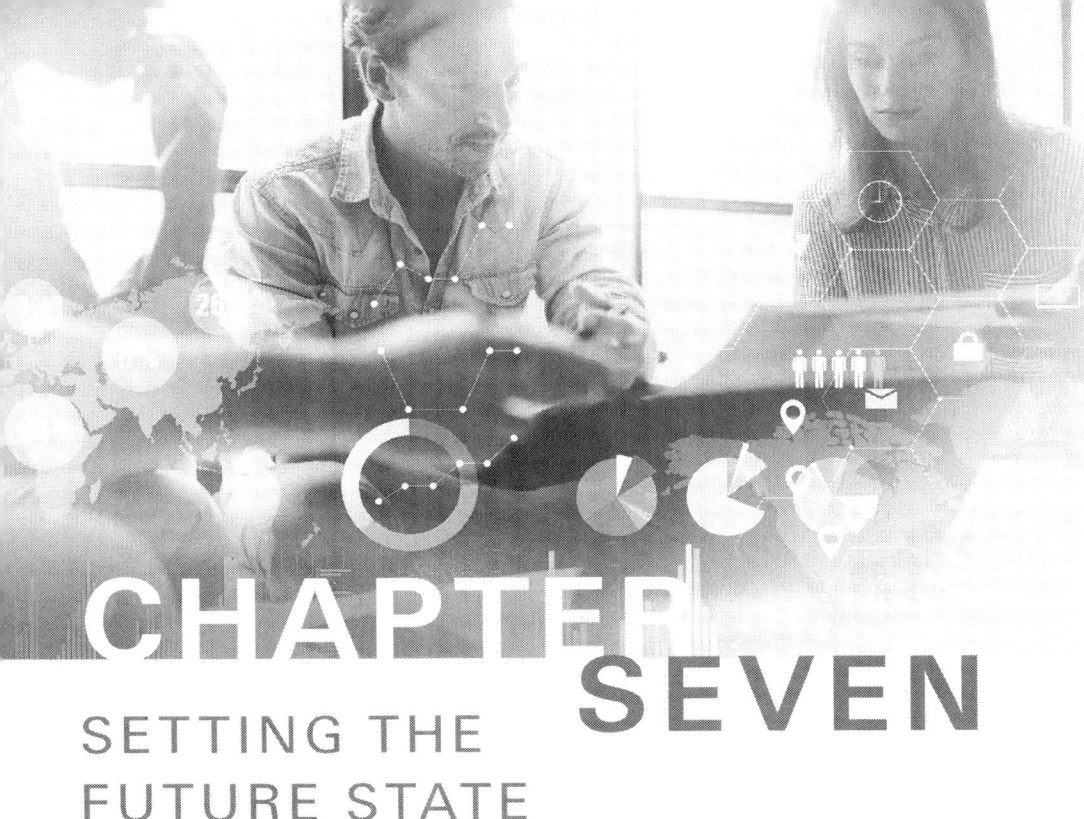

CHAPTER SEVEN

SETTING THE FUTURE STATE

As you prepare to implement your QTC solution, you are doing more than just rolling out a new piece of technology— you are setting the future state for your business. QTC has the potential to transform how employees in your company perform and manage all aspects of the sales cycle. But a new QTC system cannot by itself drive this organizational change. It's your job to define what kind of organization you want to become, then set in motion the important conversations, decision points, and feedback loops you'll need to transform your organization.

In this chapter, we're going to explore the diverse issues and nuances you will want to consider as you harness the power of QTC to conceptualize and build the future state of your business.

CPQ PROGRAM PLAN

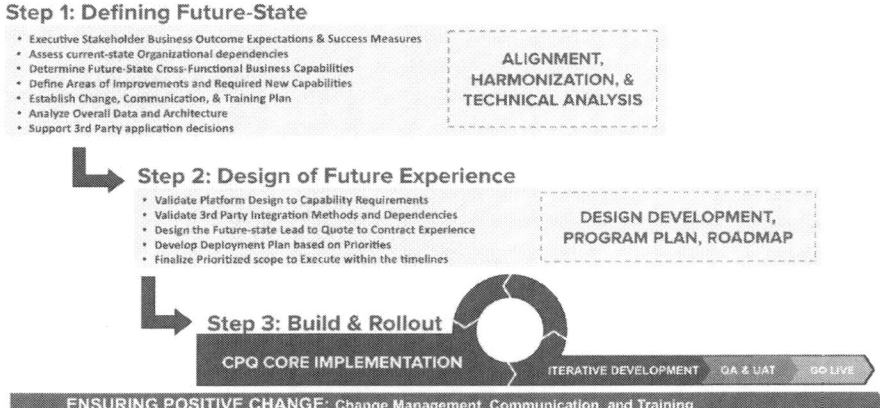

Step 1: Defining Future-State
- Executive Stakeholder Business Outcome Expectations & Success Measures
- Assess current-state Organizational dependencies
- Determine Future-State Cross-Functional Business Capabilities
- Define Areas of Improvements and Required New Capabilities
- Establish Change, Communication, & Training Plan
- Analyze Overall Data and Architecture
- Support 3rd Party application decisions

ALIGNMENT, HARMONIZATION, & TECHNICAL ANALYSIS

Step 2: Design of Future Experience
- Validate Platform Design to Capability Requirements
- Validate 3rd Party Integration Methods and Dependencies
- Design the Future-state Lead to Quote to Contract Experience
- Develop Deployment Plan based on Priorities
- Finalize Prioritized scope to Execute within the timelines

DESIGN DEVELOPMENT, PROGRAM PLAN, ROADMAP

Step 3: Build & Rollout

CPQ CORE IMPLEMENTATION   ITERATIVE DEVELOPMENT   QA & UAT   GO LIVE

ENSURING POSITIVE CHANGE: Change Management, Communication, and Training

Getting Your Processes Codified and Optimized

Most organizations preparing to implement QTC have never documented—much less evaluated—their sales lifecycle. They don't know how all of the people involved in sales-related processes have designed their workflows, nor how they've set up their ERP and other recordkeeping systems. Before you can figure out how to optimally set up QTC for your organization, you've got to figure out how all of these processes actually play out in your organization—and how you can make them better in advance of implementing QTC. Here are five key areas to focus on as you work to get your processes codified and optimized:

1. Identify and Map Your Component Relationships

Sales processes are complex and highly interdependent. You need to do more than just capture how all of your sales processes play out individually. You also should be mapping out how they interrelate as they flow through your sales cycle.

You can start with a straightforward example and linearly map every step, from identifying the customer to scoping and pricing. Then, you can build spurs off your linear path for side processes and situational processes. As you build your map, you will start to identify component relationships and dependencies. Encourage stakeholders to help you populate your map; they will be especially good at helping you identify exceptions and edge cases, which should ultimately be prioritized.

2. Agree on a Common Vocabulary

Different areas of your business likely refer to the same products, processes, and data types by different names. Depending on the world they work in, they might refer to something by its legal name, its legacy name, an internal codename, or some other shorthand. As your stakeholders get together to help you build sales process maps, it's especially important that you agree on a common vocabulary so everyone can refer to the same requirements and processes by the same name. In general, you should aim to define your processes in business terms that will be intuitively understood by every team that ultimately intersects with QTC.

3. Decide on an SKU Rationalization Strategy

SKU rationalization is an increasingly common strategy that businesses are deploying to more efficiently manage their product inventories. SKU rationalization focuses on using historical sales data to make decisions about whether to keep, reduce, or eliminate inventory. With SKU rationalization, companies weigh the costs of producing and storing a product against the potential sales of that product. Big corporations have used them to great success to quickly eliminate products before they become a bigger financial liability than an asset. As you look ahead to your QTC future, the impending rollout of your QTC solution is the perfect opportunity to think about more sophisticated, smarter ways to manage your SKUs.

4. Build Reliable, High-Quality Price Tables

Most businesses have cobbled together price books of some kind to keep track of exact prices in a systematic way, including how product prices are calculated. As you prepare for QTC implementation, you want to ensure your price data points books are reliable, comprehensive, and serving the needs of all stakeholders effectively. If you have variable pricing based on factors like market or geographic region, you should be setting up the corresponding data points for each set of customers in a market or a geographic regional custom price book for each set of customers. For example, if your domestic and international prices are different, you could create a domestic price book and a separate international price book. Be careful about the multiplication of such price books; to keep the same regional example, if you have a different price for each country, it might be better to define an adjustment factor for each country and apply that adjustment factor to a single base price book instead of using individual data points product by product.

5. Streamline and Modernize Your Product Catalog

Product catalogs in most businesses are legacy documents that have been expanded and revised unevenly and haphazardly over time. No one has comprehensively thought through how they should be structured. One of the biggest flaws of many product catalogs is how subscriptions and discounts get integrated: every time a new pricing package is put together for a customer, the business responds by creating additional SKUs. Best practices dictate that a single product should only correspond to one SKU. As you prepare for your QTC implementation, you should revisit your product catalog with an eye toward streamlining and eliminating configurations and products that do not conform to best practices.

Developing a Business Case for Implementing QTC

You may intuitively understand that you need QTC to streamline and modernize your sales processes. But that doesn't mean everyone will be on board with the change. That's why you need to develop a rock-solid business case for implementing QTC—one that will convince even your toughest critics that you'll be able to achieve a solid return on investment.

Quantify the Cost of Doing Nothing

All types of technology are often seen as a necessary expense, not a strategic investment in your future. The first thing you want to do in building a business case is to quantify the cost of doing nothing. If you can show in no uncertain terms what sales opportunities and efficiencies are being lost as a result of not having QTC, it makes the case for QTC very real—and very compelling. Try to quantify what your competition is gaining through their investment in QTC now; no company wants to be at a competitive disadvantage.

Identify Your Stakeholders' Pain Points

To build a business case that is responsive to your stakeholders' needs, it's critical that you identify a plan for solving your stakeholders' pain points using QTC. This work is as simple as sitting down with stakeholders and asking them, "What are the most cumbersome, frustrating, or inefficient parts of your job? Where do you see technology potentially helping you do your job better?"

Develop Metrics that Quantify Progress Toward Goals

Central to building a business case for QTC is having a well-defined, robust plan for tracking ROI. You should develop a variety of metrics that quantify ROI. Toward the beginning of QTC implementation, you should have some sort of metric that quantifies user adoption rates—an indication of the value that your stakeholders get out of the new system. Later on, you will need a metric that quantifies whether QTC is reducing inefficiencies, such as a lower error rate or faster processing times for key steps. Finally, you will need a metric that looks at whether QTC is leading to more sales and/or more satisfied customers, decreased average discounts/increased average margins, or similar metrics measuring the impact on the bottom line.

Have a Strategy for Achieving Stakeholder Alignment

A well-thought-out business plan offers more than just a conceptual overview of how QTC will transform your business. It also offers a tangible plan for how you will set in motion the changes you'll need to achieve your goals. In particular, you want to offer up a strategy for aligning the needs of stakeholders with QTC—and for unifying stakeholders around a shared vision of QTC success.

Developing an Implementation Roadmap for QTC

No matter how much funding you put into QTC, you cannot achieve everything all at once, nor should that be your goal. The organizational change that accompanies QTC takes time, and your strategy is likely to require some adjustments along the way.

To get the most out of your QTC investment, you will need an implementation roadmap. A roadmap offers a unified plan for when you'll implement specific capabilities and components, how you'll prioritize your finite resources, and how the components of QTC will build off one another to get you where you want to be.

Implementation roadmaps are critical for long-term success. You should develop your roadmap alongside all of your stakeholders. You not only need their buy-in and support, but you also need a document that will create long-term transparency and accountability among your stakeholders.

QTC gives you a prime opportunity to reset, redefine, and reimagine the future state of sales-related processes in your organization. Before you get started with the nuts and bolts of implementation, you should be making the most of this opportunity to get your processes codified and optimized, to develop a rock-solid business case for QTC, and to develop a QTC implementation roadmap that lays out your vision of QTC success.

CHAPTER EIGHT

CHANGE MANAGEMENT AND ADOPTION STRATEGY

Unsurprisingly, introducing any new piece of technology is going to demand some organizational change. Whether it's new processes, policy updates, or data merging, technology projects change things up and require your company culture to change too. If your culture is already conducive to accepting and successfully adopting change, tell us your secrets. What is the most common is a certain level of tug-of-war between "the way we've been doing things" to "the way we're doing it now." But if you want QTC technology to truly succeed in your organization, you'll need to prepare your people for the shift.

Organizational change management, a formal service offered by Simplus, is a perfect way to not only mediate the pains of adopting new processes and new technology but also pave the way for true widespread adoption. According to a 2016 Forrester survey, 38 percent of businesses encounter problems while implementing technology due to "slow user adoption, inadequate attention paid to change management and training, and difficulties in aligning the organizational culture with new ways of working."[1] In short, even if you do everything perfectly as far as the technical design and implementation of QTC go, you'll still struggle if the human side of change wasn't properly addressed.

This chapter will take a look at what change management and adoption strategy are, pain points associated with adoption, how change management helps, where it fits in the overall QTC journey, and best practices for rolling out change management in your organization.

Change Management and Adoption Defined

There's a difference between what change management looks like and what successful change management takes. Consider the change management iceberg: you have great organizational results that you can see, like user training, branding, UX design, user logins, and adoption surveys. But holding up those visible indicators of successful change management is a whole lot more, including the following:

- A clear future-state vision (as discussed in chapter 7)
- Defined business processes and KPIs
- Strong strategy and leadership backing
- Executive and stakeholder alignment
- Colleague morale and trust
- Organizational change competency
- User persona analysis

- Change agent network (identified individuals who will help usher in change)
- Management of change resistance
- Communication, planning, and execution
- Governance and data management

Clearly, that's much more than just user-friendly interfaces and branded training handbooks. Change management and adoption strategy require a lot more than what meets the eye. In its most successful state, your organization's approach to change management will be the process that shepherds your end users from initial hesitation to ultimate acceptance and appreciation for the coming QTC change.

And don't worry about the laundry list of everything involved in change management. With the right team behind you, it can easily be managed. But first, let's review the basic principles and goals behind change management and adoption strategy.

The Goals of Change Management and Adoption

A change management and adoption strategy is tasked with multiple end goals: awareness and engagement, training and ownership, realizing project goals, and institutionalizing the "new normal." Let's review each of these.

Awareness and Engagement

First off, change management will need to establish awareness. This doesn't mean just announcing the coming change. It's more important to confirm awareness about the need for change—the big why. Making sure end users understand the motivation for change makes the partner in this duo—engagement—much easier. After affirming awareness, change management will also strive to energize employees about the change to create the foundation for employee engagement.

Training and Ownership

This goal is one of the most obvious (and commonly mistaken as the only thing change management handles). During this step, change management practitioners will provide training materials, skill-building exercises, demonstrations, and general onboarding activities to establish the new knowledge necessary to adopt change. This will also include an emphasis on individual end-user ownership: change management should instill a sense of responsibility in each employee as buy-in and knowledge skill increases. Each time I performed end-user training for a client, questions asked by the employees were related to changes in the process rather than about how to use the new tools. This clearly demonstrates that your employees expect that you explain why you are doing this.

Realizing Project Goals

The technical goals of a QTC project take two elements to be fully realized: (1) expert technical implementation and (2) people willing and able to adopt the technology. Change management focuses on the latter and making sure the people that need to adopt the technology in order for it to be successful are primed and ready to do just that. This is done by reinforcing the change and driving optimization with new efficiencies.

Institutionalizing the "New Normal"

To any QTC project, there's the current state, and then there's the future state. Or, "what we do now" and "what we want to be doing." Part of change management is helping to institutionalize the new technology and its inherent process changes to your organization so that the future state becomes less scary and foreign and is instead easily accepted as "normal."

In addition, there are three major ROI factors behind change management efforts. It's important to be aware of these because this is how your change management leaders will be measuring the success of the overall strategy:

1. Utilization

This is a measure of how many people are on board with the coming change. For QTC, it means how many of your designated end users are ready to transition to new tools like CPQ, CLM, and billing.

2. Speed of Adoption

Speed of adoption is simply a way of capturing how quickly those end users get on board with the new tools. Does it take one week? Two? A month? Longer?

3. Proficiency

This is perhaps the most telling ROI metric behind change management. Proficiency means how much improvement occurs after the change has been adopted and users are on board. The more adoption, the more proficiency rises.

The Big Misconception Behind Change Management

There is one big misconception that should be cleared up before you start change management and your larger QTC journey: change management is not a separate process or a single assigned resource. Too often, organizations see the technical project as a big looming bubble, and then to the side is a smaller organizational change management resource ready to support as needed.

The trouble is, nothing about change management should be on an "as needed" basis. Change management is always needed, and even in the best corporate cultures and organizations, projects with change management efforts yield better results than projects without. Change management resources should be intimately involved in the entire project, not tacked on at the end. They should understand the beginning, middle, and ultimate end goals of a project. They should be responsible for a given portion of the project's KPIs, i.e., the ones that are dependent on people and change adoption.

Adoption Pain Points

So what motivates all this effort in change management? You probably know it intuitively from previous change efforts in your organization, but can't quite put it into words. Doubts, resistance, lack of knowledge, and poor ROI on the ultimate project goals are all linked to QTC projects that went without clear change management. Other pain points associated with not leveraging change management go much further than just the QTC project alone:

- Lack of stakeholder engagement
- Unclear communication

- No set expectations from end users
- Siloed departments and systems
- Active and passive resistance
- Lack of user adoption
- Employee turnover
- Stalled improvement
- Less benefit realization
- Lower ROI or poor methodology to track ROI

All QTC projects begin at the current state and envision landing at the ideal future state for their given goals and tools implemented. But on the way there, many fall off track or get to the future state with a lot of pain and tears along the way. There are three basic scenarios a project can follow based on the state of change management involvement:

1. Change begins, followed by a brief transition period, return equilibrium reached on time, and ROI is realized ahead of schedule and in greater return than expected.

2. Change begins, followed by a lengthy transition period with no return equilibrium ever reached, and ROI is realized eventually.

3. Change begins, followed by no transition period, and no ROI is realized.

It's not hard to pick out which scenario you want to be: #1. This is the scenario where change management is embraced and done right. Scenario #2 is when change management is involved but done poorly. And finally, #3 is the "valley of despair" that strikes organizations with no change management efforts on their projects.

But a proper strategy can ensure neither of the latter two scenarios plagues your project.

How Change Management Helps

What Projects Need Change Management?

There is rarely a project that does not benefit from change management. If technology and change are involved, having a clear strategy on your side will almost certainly guarantee better results, happier end users, and satisfied executives. Since QTC is a multifaceted journey that touches various departments and affects the bottom line of your organization so pointedly, it's no wonder that a majority of QTC projects impact business processes.

What Departments Benefit from Change Management?

It's easy to see how a project begins to affect multiple departments, functional roles, and user personas—all of which need a change management practitioner ready to work with them. In QTC projects, sales is the most heavily impacted department, followed by IT, finance, human resources, legal, and marketing. Measuring the level of impact felt in each department or by each individual is a matter of analyzing how the anticipated changes will affect each area's compensation, performance reviews, structure, mindset, behaviors, job roles, tools, systems, and processes. Depending on the particulars of your QTC project, change may hit each department differently. But one thing is sure: it will hit.

Specific Benefits from Effective Change Management

The biggest umbrella benefit motivating your entire change management effort is the expectation that project objectives will be met more effectively, quickly, and happily. In fact, companies that apply a comprehensive organizational change management program are six times more likely to meet or exceed project objectives. Those with change management in the top tier ("excellent") meet 93 percent of project objectives. Compared to "poor" change management projects coming in at 15 percent met objectives, that's a difference of 78 percent.[2]

Change management is crucial for several other reasons:

- Clear communication lines
- Collaborative departments and synced-up systems
- Acceptance and excitement about the change
- Increase in colleague trust and morale
- Sped-up proficiency, adoption, and ROI realization
- Less employee turnover

Now that we have an in-depth understanding of what change management is, the pain points it addresses, and the benefits it yields during QTC projects, that leads to the next big question: when should change management take shape during your QTC journey?

Where Change Management Fits in the QTC Journey

According to Jean-Baptiste Minchelli, senior director of product management, Lightning enablement, and adoption at Salesforce,

> It doesn't matter how great your Salesforce solution is if users don't—or won't—use it. It's not enough to just give your team a great app, you also need to train, support, and give them a sound reason to adopt it. In other words, you need to plan your rollout strategy just as carefully as you planned design, development, and testing.[3]

I've said it before and I'll say it again: change takes time, so it makes sense that you should start planning your change management and adoption strategy early on in the stages of a QTC project, with just as much care as the technical side of the project. While new technology is implemented in the hopes of making internal processes faster and easier, it doesn't always. In fact, user engagement with new technologies isn't rising at many organizations. In a 2015 survey, Knoa Software found that only 8.4 percent of enterprise software errors were "system-related"; 91.6 percent of errors were "related to the user, design or process."[4] When the people handling the technology aren't truly engaged with it, adoption never sticks.

This is why it's so critical to put the planning behind user enablement, onboarding, and adoption—change management as a whole—at the start of any given QTC project. You increase the odds of project success and adoption when planning for change management in the beginning. This is why Simplus recommends planning for change management as soon as possible.

From the very beginning, when the change is being introduced, you will have to prove to your employees why the new QTC tools are worth the investment, what they do, and how they work on a very specific, granular level that leaves an impression on each user persona. If you don't, they'll either continue using the tools and processes they're comfortable with or corrupt the one you're trying to implement.

But with a carefully planned change management and adoption strategy guiding your project from the start, QTC can take off. When Simplus worked with Mitsubishi Electric Automotive America, our change management team oversaw the training and onboarding of MEAA end users. Through advisory and discovery sessions and diligent work, this resulted in 30 percent more approved opportunities and 95 percent faster quote delivery.[5] It was all thanks to users truly understanding and adopting the QTC tools.

How to Roll Out Change Management and Your Adoption Strategy

QTC technology requires change and a cultural shift to be adopted in any organization. And Salesforce knows it. In fact, Salesforce resources warn that

> if leadership is not committed to an organizational initiative, that initiative will fail. . . . The best way to demonstrate this commitment is by example. This is also where you want to start: at the top.[6]

Rolling out change management and your overall adoption strategy for QTC will require, first and foremost, executive alignment and support. Once that is secured, the rest of the rollout moves along easily.

CHANGE SUCCESS: METHODOLOGY

Leverage a robust playbook to plan, lead, and manage the human side of implementing strategic change and the adoption of CRM cloud solutions.

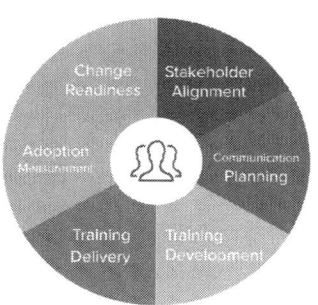

1. Change Readiness
- Organizational readiness
- Identify barriers to change
- Stakeholder analysis
- Adoption metrics
- Change management plan

2. Stakeholder Alignment
- Leadership visioning
- Business champions
- Change agent network
- Leadership and manager coaching

3. Communication Planning
- Communication plan with activities, channels, owners, and deliverables
- Value-based messaging
- Communication execution

4. Training Development
- Training analysis and plan
- Curriculum development
- Persona- and process-based content
- Content outputs

5. Training Delivery
- End-user training execution and delivery
- Train the Trainer program
- Training support and post learning
- Training evaluation

6. Adoption Measurement
- Conduct adoption assessment
- Measure adoption via defined metrics
- Refine change plan based on adoption results

Best Practices

Here are some tried and true best practices for securing that executive alignment and rolling out change management for the QTC journey:

1. Distinguish project management (structuring the technical side of change) and sponsorship (executive leadership and governance) from change management (managing the people side of change).

2. Understand that change management is a process that works on both an organizational and individual level. For the organization, this means preparing, managing, and reinforcing the change. On an individual level, ADKAR is the Prosci industry standard for lasting change management.

    a. Awareness

    b. Desire

    c. Knowledge

    d. Ability

    e. Reinforcement[7]

3. Take advantage of all available training resources. At Simplus, we offer train-the-trainer sessions, end-user training packages, virtual training, eLearning videos, and training database management.

4. When evaluating change readiness, be sure to honestly analyze the current state and identify the barriers and risks to change. Incorporate leadership visioning during this stage to make sure executive alignment is maintained.

Phases and Activities

Change management is intimately involved in each stage of the QTC journey. Here's a look at some of the specific activities change management practitioners will undertake during each stage:

Mobilization

- Hold stakeholder interviews
- Conduct leadership visioning
- Present a readiness survey
- Host change workshops
- Identify change barriers, risks to change

Setting the Future State

- Establish a change agent network
- Hold executive and manager coaching
- Manage resistance
- Understand requirements
- Host day-in-the-life scenarios
- Conduct knowledge transfer on business processes
- Attend sprint demos
- Gather training collateral
- Identify skill gaps

Implementation

- Continue executive and manager coaching
- Work with change agent network to promote change
- Manage resistance

- Understand requirements
- Host day-in-the-life scenarios
- Conduct knowledge transfer on business processes
- Attend sprint demos
- Gather training collateral
- Identify skill gaps

QA

- Continue executive and manager coaching
- Work with change agent network to promote change
- Manage resistance
- Plan logistics for training and develop curriculum
- Alpha, beta, and final reviews

Rollout, Integration, and Beyond

- Continue executive and manager coaching
- Work with change agent network to promote change
- Manage resistance
- Hold training evaluations
- Present adoption surveys
- Offer additional training support
- Roll out incentive programs
- Gather feedback
- Reinforce change

Tools

In addition to these best practices followed by our change management team, there are specific materials and tools your organization will likely need to employ to realize the benefits of QTC through change management:

- A readiness assessment
- Communications plan
- Sponsor roadmap
- Coaching plan
- Resistance management
- Training plan

Preparing for Adoption from the Outset

At this point, you should understand that preparing for the change in your business and for adoption by your employees is a critical task that should be started as early as possible in your QTC journey. Here are some practical tips and insights:

- Define company-wide policies. Exceptions to the rules are the enemy to simplification. Mitigate exceptions with approvals, not with attempts at automation.
- Enforce consistency in processes and encourage automation opportunities.
- Make it easy for your clients and partners to do business with you, as they will also be your system users through communities and portals.
- A good user experience is critical.
- Through all phases of the project, get contribution from a small group of future champion users: those who are vocally looking for change and that others will follow.
- Ensure that key stakeholders are visible supporters of the changes in process and in technology.
- Maintain visual checkpoints throughout the entire project.

- Start the hype from day one and build excitement.
- Be clear about why this is happening.

Change management for the QTC journey is crucial for ultimate success with CPQ, CLM, billing, and the entire quote-to-cash process. By considering your change management and adoption strategy early on—from the very beginning, even—and attentively taking care of the people side of change, you can ensure greater understanding, acceptance, and use of QTC tools.

CHAPTER NINE

IMPLEMENTATION METHODOLOGY

When the time comes to implement QTC, you cannot simply turn over responsibility for implementation to a seasoned QTC implementation consultant and let them do the rest. To get the outcomes you desire, you need to be a proactive partner working alongside your QTC consultant every step of the way. The goal isn't for you to do the work of your implementation consultant; rather, it's to provide your consultant with a critical perspective and insights about your organization itself. You need to communicate your organization's priorities, serve as a liaison and a spokesperson for your stakeholders, and help your consultant understand the sensibilities, preferences, and nuances of your stakeholders.

To collaborate effectively with your QTC consultant, you also need to understand what they will need from you and what they will lean on you to provide. The goal of this chapter is to walk you through how a seasoned QTC consultant will do their job. The more you can get into the mindset, pacing, and sensibilities of your consultant, the more effectively you'll be positioned to work alongside them.

IMPLEMENTATION METHODOLOGY

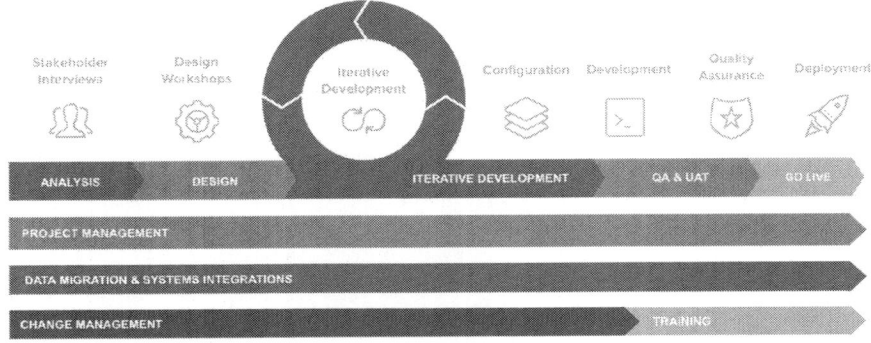

What Not to Do

While considering methodologies, you may already have one or another in mind. Agile and Waterfall are, after all, the most popular implementation methodologies in the market. However, when it comes to QTC implementation, neither is truly up for the task. Let's examine each and go over why they fail to measure up.

A Pure Agile Approach

Agile, as its name implies, is all about speed and dexterity. In Agile, focus is placed on small teams that organize themselves, not by tasks, but by time. Teams are responsible for organizing their work into clearly defined periods of time—called "sprints"—to which they assign a list of deliverables. When organizing the sprint, teams work closely with clients to determine/prioritize deliverables based on business value.

At the end of the sprint, the most important deliverables have been completed. If any tasks have not been completed, they are those that the client deemed less important, and the client and team reprioritize work for the coming sprint.

Though many prefer Agile for its emphasis on client involvement, a pure Agile approach is not ideal. For one, not all clients want to be as involved as Agile methodology demands. Further, Agile fails to fully consider the future state. For example, if the future state indicates that ramp/escalator deals will be part of the solution, there is a significant impact on bundle design as well as pricing design. However, an Agile methodology might not identify these needs early enough to make an impact. If that was the case, the amount of rework at the design level would be gigantic.

Waterfall

Waterfall, also known as traditional methodology, is a very linear approach to projects, with every project typically divided into seven stages:

- Requirements specification
- Design
- Construction
- Integration
- Testing
- Installation
- Maintenance

When using this methodology, every stage is kept distinct and without overlap, and client approval is necessary before moving on to the next stage. While this may seem to ensure that requirements are met because they are set early on, there isn't much room left for discovery. At the end of the project, clients may realize that what they wanted isn't what was best. Even worse, there is no feedback collected from the end user until at least UAT. Any feedback provided by the end user is at risk of compromising the current design approach for the entire solution. These realizations come at a point when it is the most expensive to correct.

The Hybrid Methodology

The ideal approach combines aspects of Agile and Waterfall into a new methodology perfect for ensuring your QTC implementation's success: the Hybrid. Before its acquisition by Salesforce, SteelBrick used Hybrid Methodology through hundreds of successful projects. To this day, Simplus uses an enhanced Hybrid Methodology to ensure project success for its clients worldwide. So let's go over the Hybrid Methodology and its four main steps: analysis and design, build and development, testing, and deployment.

SAMPLE IMPLEMENTATION APPROACH

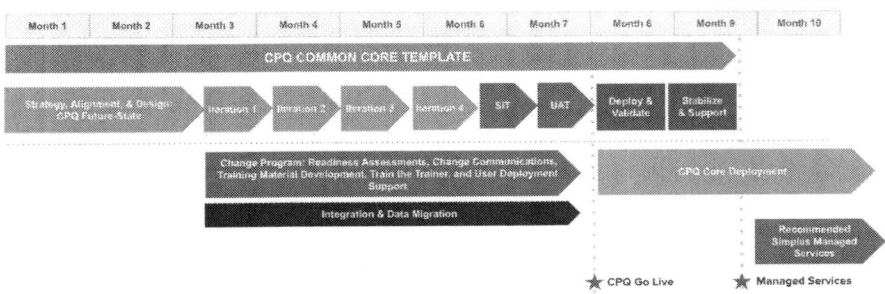

Analysis and Design

Analysis and design must take place as early as possible. For example, you can start by asking yourself these questions:

- Do we understand what the catalog needs to look like and how products and services can be combined together as viable end customer solutions?
- Do we know what the pricing and discounting strategies, policies, and models are?
- Have we defined approval authorities and corresponding processes for the types of transactions that the business needs to execute?

The outcome of A&D needs to be digestible by business users, IT people, and people who don't understand QTC. To that end, you need to be able to paint a picture and tell a story. Yes, you can have supporting documents that get into more technical detail, but the primary documents should paint a picture that a layman can understand and that you can include in user stories.

Most importantly, the workshops and discussions throughout the analysis and design phase must cover the entire future state, well beyond the scope of the first phase of the QTC journey. This approach allows the QTC architect to build a solid foundation for the solution from the ground up.

Build and Development

The keyword of the build and development phase is "iteration," as in "the repetition of a process or utterance." The iterative build process breaks the work down into iterations or chunks of work. Now, unlike with other clouds, you can't always drive sequencing by priority. Best practices dictate that you start with foundational iterations—often the most technically complex pieces—first before moving on to the more simple.

The major goal in the build phase is to be able to do multiple show-and-tell sessions. These will give you the insight you need to course-correct carefully and early. With CPQ more than other clouds, there aren't as many paths to correct implementation (e.g., products must come before pricing, but they remain dependent on each other).

In the next section, we will present testing, but keep in mind that unit testing should be performed by the build and development resources and is therefore an inherent part of the build phase. At the same time, each iteration is an opportunity to get feedback from future users, and it is highly encouraged to organize a mini user acceptance testing session at the end of such iterations.

Testing

Which form of testing will you use? In addition to unit testing—once again, performed during the build phase—the following types of testing should be considered:

- **Functional Testing:** Testing user stories and their acceptance criteria
- **System Integration Testing:** Testing integration between the QTC solution and other systems
- **End-to-End Testing:** Testing that business processes are tying user stories together, from beginning to end
- **User Acceptance Testing:** Testing how future end users engage with the product

Of all of these options, user acceptance testing is the most important, and it usually comes as the final stage. This is where you truly take ownership. In this stage, you should be executing your test scripts and be relatively aligned with what you build. The greatest challenge with user acceptance testing is that customers bring in a different group of people with new points of view. Inevitably, these will throw wrenches into the process. The feedback collected from future users during UAT should be documented and carefully prioritized.

We will go into greater detail in chapter 10.

Deployment

Once testing is complete and has gone well (i.e., you have a "Go" decision from your Go/No-Go team), the time has come to move on to deployment. Deployment is the means by which everything that makes your QTC processes function technically gets transferred over to the next environment, ultimately into the production environment for go-live. It can get complicated and intimidatingly technical very quickly, so we'll go into more detail on this step in chapter 11. Suffice it to say for now that every project will have its own deployment list which it follows based on customizations, declarative configuration, and data we need to load.

CHAPTER TEN

QA STRATEGY

William A. Foster, a decorated soldier of WWII who threw himself on a grenade to save his fellow Marines, is often quoted as saying,

> Quality is never an accident; it is always the result of high intention, sincere effort, intelligent direction and skillful execution. It represents the wise choice of many alternatives, the cumulative experience of many masters of craftsmanship; and it also marks the quest of an ideal after necessity has been satisfied and usefulness achieved.

Except that Foster never actually said these words. As a factory worker before the war, Foster never would have had occasion to deliver such an address before dying in the Battle of Okinawa in 1945. No, they were actually delivered by the similarly named Will A. Foster of the Gabel-Risdon Creamery Co. in an address before the International Association of Milk Dealers in or around 1930. And even then, it is unclear whether Foster the creamery man wrote the definition himself or was quoting yet another source. Regardless, a simple coincidence of name has led to the quote being misattributed over and over again, with few ever catching on to the mistake.[1]

The misattribution actually helps to underscore the truth of the quote. Quality indeed requires careful, sincere effort. Though tempting, you can never allow yourself to assume your product's quality. In this chapter, we will discuss the importance of the quality assurance process, how to plan for it, and the steps of its execution.

Quality Assurance Strategy

Quality assurance, as you may already be aware, is the ongoing practice of testing your products and established processes in order to detect and resolve problems and ultimately reduce risk. By conducting quality assurance (QA), you ensure your customers a safe, easy, intuitive, and overall positive experience.

The core of successful QA is to plan early. If you start thinking about QA during UAT (user acceptance testing) or SIT (system integration testing), it's already too late. Instead, quality must be considered from the earliest stages: design and build.

Design

When beginning the design processes, many companies make the mistake of focusing on implementation and ignoring adoption—i.e., they focus on delivering the good or service and forget about customer interaction with it. Keep your customers in mind, though, and you'll find that the QA process goes much more smoothly. You can do this by following these tips:

1. Ask, "Why did we build this?"

The system design must reflect the "why." Otherwise, there will be confusion, frustration, and a lack of adoption.

2. Simplify your processes.

Define your company-wide policies; the more defined they are, the less room for error you'll encounter. Remember, exceptions to the rules are the enemy to simplification, so enforce consistency wherever you can. The simpler you keep it, the easier it will be to provide an intimately intuitive experience for your users. If you plan to enable self-service for your customers and partners through communities and portals, don't forget that such external users will not have the opportunity to be trained on how to use the system. Without an intuitive experience, they will perceive that it's difficult to do business with you.

3. Streamline ease of use and compliance by involving sales reps.

Good user experience is critical, and no one knows more about delivering one than your sales reps. They know what your customers want and how they want it delivered, so involve them in the design process as much as you can. You'll find that this will eliminate guesswork on the part of your designers.

Also, keep in mind that the cost of fixing a problem at the design stage is about 100 times less than discovering it and fixing it at Go Live.

Build

Rather than keep the build process isolated, include your company as much as you can. You can do this by following these tips:

1. **Prepare the organization.**

As soon as you begin building, start broadcasting that change is coming. Ensure that key stakeholders are visible supporters, and start asking for regional helpers to assist in user acceptance testing, or see if your champion reps are available. Analyze dependent processes and systems to make sure they are ready for the change.

2. **Maintain visual checkpoints.**

Make checkpoints a priority; the earlier you can see the solution under development, the sooner you can assess usability, process fit, etc. Include your sales team in the checkpoints so they can give you their first impressions.

If you follow best practices in terms of QTC implementation methodology, you will have opted for an iterative build phase. Each iteration is an opportunity to showcase what you have built so far and test it with actual future users of the system. Collecting feedback during build gives you the possibility to address identified problems and to evaluate suggestions received at a much earlier stage than if you waited for the official UAT phase.

Planning for QA

User Stories

Essential to your QA strategy are user stories. A user story is a tool used to embody a product or service feature from an end-user perspective; its objective is to express a business requirement (i.e., piece of functionality the end user wants to have). Composed properly, a user story describes three things:

1. Who the user is
2. What the user wants
3. Why the user wants it

As you build user stories—which happens early on during analysis and design—you need to define success criteria for them. Those success criteria become the key elements to test for; if you pass those success criteria, your user story passes as well:

- Being able to quote a specific product
- Being able to quote a specific bundle made of XYZ components
- Quote a product to a specific customer at the correct price based on volume and term

Some user stories will be high level (e.g., "I need to be able to add products to my quote"). But this high level is not very useful. For example, if you were to add a product on a quote, then you would also need to get the correct customer-specific prices based on quantity purchased. Success criteria are now system-driven volume and/or term discounts and customer-specific pricing, which is highly complex and can be implemented in different manners. What is important is not the design of the solution, but the expected outcome of the story.

Test Cases

After creating your user stories and success criteria, it is time to create test cases. You should have at least one test case per success criteria, though one user story may have many success criteria, and each one of them can lead to multiple test cases.

Simply put, a test case describes a stimulus (such as an action, input, or event) and the expected response. In the next section, we'll go into the process of how test cases are used.

Different Kinds of Tests

Functional Testing: In functional testing, action is more important than form. Essentially, you test the functions of your program to see what input creates what output.

System Integration Testing (SIT): SIT is the testing of a complete system, ensuring that all of the interconnected parts (be they hardware, software, etc.) are functioning together properly.

End-to-End Testing: Here, you take a system through its entire process, beginning to end, ensuring there are no hiccups or missed connections along the way.

User Acceptance Testing (UAT): This is the final phase of any testing process. Here, you will allow your intended users to take a crack at your system, making sure it can do everything they want it to do for them.

QA Steps

1. Create a positive test case.

The purpose of a positive test case is to verify that normal use of the system leads to the desired and expected outcome. For example, you might have a user story in which a user requires that all list prices be in the price book. As part of this user story, you would say if you do have a list price in the price book, you are able to quote the product with that list price.

2. Create a negative test case.

The purpose of the test case is to prove that, under specific conditions, you may not meet success criteria. For example, you might have a user story in which a user requires that all list prices be in the price book. As part of this user story, you would say that if you don't have a list price, you should not be able to quote a product. You would have to do a negative test case where you create a product without a price book entry and verify that you cannot quote the product.

3. Create a test script.

A test script is a set of step-by-step instructions of what a tester has to do to run the test case. There are two different types of test scripts:

Open

An open test script is similar to the test case narrative. The key to an open test is that the testers are free to do whatever they want, under some high-level guidance; their end goal is to try to break the application. To that end, testers select a product without you telling them which one, choose the quantity, apply a discretionary discount (again, without specifying which one), and verify that they have obtained the expected net price (without you telling them what the net price and total should be). As another example, you may have them choose three different bundles and try to quote something that is not acceptable.

Closed

In a closed test script, testers follow rigid instructions to arrive at specific conclusions. You will tell them exactly what to do, which product to add, what quantity to specify, and what net price and total price to expect for specified values. As another example, you may want testers to verify that if they select option 1, they cannot also include option 2 in bundle XYZ. There is no longer any room for guessing for the tester. They should get exactly those results you intend for them in order to pass the test.

Be as granular as needed in these test cases to make sure you cover the complexities of your implementation. This is especially true when testing against complex product dependencies or complex pricing models or logic, or verifying that specific approvals are triggered under specific conditions. Remember to include negative closed tests in your plan.

4. Define how much coverage you want to have.

By coverage, we mean the percentage of application functionality in the user story you want to verify as part of the testing effort. It is highly unlikely you will be able to achieve 100 percent coverage. After all, you won't have enough time to write and run all of the necessary test scripts. So within your company, you'll need to estimate an acceptable test coverage. The typical recommendation is to reach at least 75 percent coverage.

5. Have resources who can work on test cases and test scripts.

Test cases and test scripts are typically done by business analysts or QA specialists. This is because the process can be very time-consuming; the last thing you want is to assign the work to employees whose time would be better spent on tasks they specialize in. So have your analysts and specialists begin work as soon as possible. In order to keep pace with the validation of user stories, don't wait for all of the user stories to come in at once. Start as soon as you receive them. Keep in mind that user stories might evolve during your project, and put in place a process to adjust test cases and test scripts accordingly.

6. Plan for SIT and UAT phases.

Select your testers ahead of time.

For UAT, the testers should be end users or future end users. SIT can be tested by the core team before you open to future users in UAT. SIT is usually technical, so expect IT to be heavily involved.

Plan how testing will be executed.

There's no single right way to execute testing. You could always establish a schedule in which time is taken out of every day and devoted to testing (e.g., one hour a day for five weeks). Or you could try to get everything done at once by locking your team in a room and keeping them there until the testing is complete. Both approaches work, but even with the second option, it would be impossible to resolve everything in a single session: you would still need to wait a few days for the team to fix reported problems before you could move on to the next round of testing. You might lock testers for in a room for two days and give them three days back, then repeat the process the following week. And if you were to use the hourly method, you would need to be sure those users understand that they have to contribute time to testing every day so that the team can fix the bugs and verify the fixes hold up. Prepare a schedule to document who tests which test script. For some test scripts, have multiple testers execute them, especially open scripts, to ensure you get different feedback from different individuals when it comes to user experience.

Use precise tracking.

Be sure to track which test cases and test scripts you have executed, which ones failed and passed, which ones passed when fixed, etc. Keep in mind that you will have a lot to track, and doing everything through spreadsheets will be painful, to say the least. That's why we highly recommend using advanced tools for tracking, such as Jira.

Prioritize.

When treating failed test scripts and test cases, make sure to report problems precisely. Educate and train the testers on how and what to report.

As problems are reported, know how to rate them so that the most important problems get fixed before the others. You may consider using a rating system such as the following:

P0 = critical

P1 = important

P2 = medium

P3 = low

As part of your rating system, you may decide that some errors are acceptable when going live. But you still need to define which priority level must be fixed before you go live. You may have 75 percent overall coverage, but if you have any P0 or P1 problem, you may not want to go live at all. It's not just the quantity: it's also the quality. By prioritizing each reported issue, you can incorporate the quality aspect of the exercise.

Establish a go/no-go process.

You need to verify how much coverage you have obtained. Maybe you wanted 75 percent but only achieved 70 percent. Now, this doesn't mean you won't move forward to go-live— but you need a team that will make that go/no-go decision.

For example, you may say you want 75 percent coverage and no P0 or P1 issues. The team will verify that these criteria are met and give the green light. Once you are organized, the team's work will be straightforward.

Remember that having your user stories and corresponding success criteria ready early on for the build phase will make the build process much more efficient, as your build resources will be able to perform unit testing based on these user stories and verify that success criteria are met.

CHAPTER ELEVEN

DEPLOYMENT STRATEGY

Throughout your QTC journey, and especially during the implementation project for QTC tools like CPQ, deployment will be a repeating concern. It's that time when all the data and functionality has to move from one environment to another, such as from development to testing, and then perhaps back to development, followed by another round of testing. And, eventually, from testing to production.

Deployment is the means by which everything that makes your QTC processes function technically gets transferred over to the next environment. It can get complicated and intimidatingly technical very quickly, but this chapter is here to break it down more simply and explain what you can do to manage the process with as little headache as possible.

Deployment Defined

Deployment for QTC is more than just the final migration to the production environment. If it's not that simple, you may be wondering what more it involves.

Well, if we go back to the implementation methodology for QTC, we know that the recommended build is iterative. This means that at the end of each iteration, you will organize show-and-tell and mini-UAT sessions with testers to provide feedback and identify issues. Such sessions are usually done in a testing environment, and you will need to deploy the latest version of your solution to that environment.

In modern applications like Salesforce CPQ, implementation itself is a combination of code, metadata, and reference data—all of which will have to go through that testing, as covered in chapter 10. Salesforce provides the tools to migrate some of that information: code and metadata. However, *reference data* can only be migrated with traditional data export and import operations. This is where migration and deployment vendors like Prodly Moover come in. Without these tools, deployment becomes a major pain point that can potentially hold up your entire project.

A relational data migration tool such as Prodly Moover is perfect for avoiding that situation. Relational data migration means maintaining the parent-child relationships between multiple objects, levels, relationships, and records between Salesforce orgs. Since your project will involve multiple orgs in different stages or environments, maintaining these crucial relationships throughout the journey is imperative for true, clean testing and ultimately for a solution that matches what you're expecting.

Deployment Pain Points

Since tools like Salesforce CPQ or Salesforce Billing are largely dependent on interrelated reference data, migrating reference data correctly is extremely important. A basic data loader application allows you to deploy objects containing the reference data one object at a time. Preserving the relationship between these objects is error-prone and cumbersome, as it remains a manual step. In fact, using a data loader application may alter the state of your project entirely. A QTC implementation done without proper deployment suffers from

- stalled implementation,
- corrupted test environments,
- unscalable, unreliable, and unrepeatable QTC updates, and
- weak business agility.

Benefits of Automated Deployments

Prodly Moover provides a proven and easy-to-use tool to mitigate those risks and migrate reference data the right way during QTC project implementations. At its core, the advantage of using a deployment tool like Moover is the ability to replace your project's manual, spreadsheet-riddled data loader process with an easy-to-use, fully automated, and native app on the Salesforce platform.

In addition to the overarching peace of mind a reference data migration tool like Prodly Moover offers, proper deployment also gives your QTC project these added benefits:

- Decrease in migration work time
- Repeatable, scalable, and no- or low-touch migrations

- Increased developer productivity
- Ensured business-critical revenue
- On-time project delivery
- More realized value from your QTC investment

Finally, Prodly Moover also comes with a prebuilt set of templates for CPQ that I personally created. This template is designed to set your deployment strategy off right and encourage best practices along the way.

Best Practices for Deployment

Deployment is understandably a scary time in the QTC journey—transitioning all the hard work to environments that are increasingly close to the final, live solution. But there are several tips and tricks to handle deployment like a pro and alleviate the stress.

Manage Environments with Care

Best practice dictates that testing should not be done in the same environment as development. This is to avoid conflicts and confusion while design is still being revised, because if you break something as you are currently developing, then you can't test anymore.

This means that you have to deploy a stable version of your implemented solutions from a development environment to a test environment; and then from there, potentially to a training environment if you choose to leverage one of these as part of your adoption strategy; and finally, to a staging environment. A staging environment contains the last, fully tested, next version of the production environment. As your QTC solution makes its way through each of these environments, it's important that the distinction between each environment is maintained. Corrupt your environments, and you may lose key reference data along the way. But if you keep each of these environments clearly distinguished from the others and manage them with care, deployment runs seamlessly.

Typical implementation environments are as follows:

1. Development
2. Testing
3. Training
4. Staging
5. Production (live)

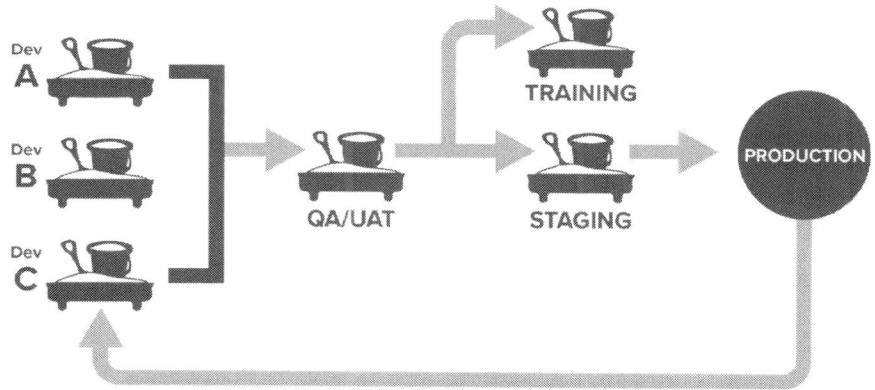

Additionally, when you implement the solution, you will likely have to execute migrations between these environments multiple times—at a minimum, once per iteration during the build phase. Because of this, the deployment structure between environments should be considered and planned for early on to ensure that you respect your internal IT policies.

Follow a Predeployment Checklist

In my experience, a predeployment checklist is helpful for guaranteeing the most successful and clean migration of your

CPQ data. In collaboration with Prodly Moover, I've compiled this checklist to guide organizations preparing for deployment in a QTC project:

- Ensure CPQ versions match in source and destination.
- Ensure schemas match (if not, do a change set).
- Clean up source records to eliminate duplicates.
- Ensure deployment users have a CPQ license in destination (if necessary).
- Disable CPQ triggers (single switch) in destination.
- Determine best UPSERT method.
- Use appropriate CPQ data set templates, and adjust them as necessary for your company if you use CEIDs (composite external IDs) to ensure they are unique.
- Document carefully and exhaustively manual deployment tasks (such as environment-dependent URLs or Salesforce IDs stored in text fields).

Abide by Prodly's Data Set Deployment Sequence

Finally, for best results, you should also follow a best practice for deployment sequencing. With Prodly's experience and expertise, we have put together a certain order suggested for deployment. Following this sequence minimizes the risk of corrupted reference data and alleviates migration stress.

1. Price books
2. Products
3. Price rule
4. Product rule
5. Localization
6. Quote templates
7. Remaining info can be done in parallel

After deploying in this order, be sure to turn CPQ triggers back on in the destination org.

With the right approach, the right tools, and the right partner, deployment can be an easy step in your QTC journey. Simplus and Prodly Moover are experts in migrating CPQ reference data throughout your project, and we know how to use best practices along the way. Then, once your deployment strategy is in place, it's time to consider the next big step in your journey: rollout.

CHAPTER TWELVE

ROLLOUT STRATEGY

How do we define rollout? It's primarily about choosing who will be the users for the next release of the CPQ or QTC project. At the end of the day, it's about prioritization. Let's put some context around how we can go through that prioritization.

The most successful CPQ projects are those that start simple. It's the 80/20 rule: pick 20 percent of user stories that address 80 percent of the needs of the business. We can give a list of bullet points of criteria to consider for making that threshold decision.

Phased vs. Big-Bang Rollout

As you decide this, focus on your company's growth strategy and align the rollout accordingly. In general, you have two main options when it comes to your rollout: phased or big bang.

Phased Rollout

Phased rollout is a method in which rollout is done in steps. Rather than execute rollout across an entire organization in facets of the final vision, it is done piece by piece.

For example, Hitachi Vantara's business relied primarily on renewals. That is why when they partnered with Salesforce, their first order of business was to roll out a reinvented renewals process before moving on to new products.[1] That may not make sense for your organization, and that's exactly the point: no two businesses are exactly alike, so don't look for a one-size-fits-all solution. Here are some ways you may stage your rollout.

By Product Line/Business Unit

If you acquire a company, you may need more time to unify the new organization's processes to match the parent company. In this case, you would delay the implementation of a new product line until they are ready. Instead, you might want to start with a focus on SaaS and grow the SaaS model. Two or three years later, if you need the brick-and-mortar business, you can implement at that time.

By Region/Market

Let's say you are a global company whose processes are maturing in North America. However, your processes in Europe, the Middle East, and Africa are struggling. Given the nature of the EMEA market, every country will have its own way of doing business. If you cannot agree on a single simplified process, the implementation will be more complex and take a lot more time. In this case, you would roll out by region, market area, or geographic area.

By Sales Channel

You may need to prioritize channel partners over internal sales representatives or vice versa. Once you have a robust implementation for your internal organization, move on to the community portal.

By Functionality

You could do CPQ but delay doing CLM, billing, or integrations. You could even focus on the P and Q without doing the C first.

By Type of Transaction

Start with new business deals and later address add-on sales and renewals.

When the rollout is executed in phases, you allow your organization time to adjust and become acclimated to changes over time, resulting in less pushback. Think of it like dipping your toes in a pool of cold water versus jumping straight in: you reduce the shock and give your employees and teams an idea of what they're in for.

In addition, you're protecting yourself from disaster and empowering yourself. When rollout is handled in stages, problems related to implementation likewise arise in stages instead of all at once. And as you continue your rollout, the lessons you learn along the way can prevent more problems further down the process, meaning fewer problems in the overall execution.

However, having groups of users working with different systems or employees working with elements of different systems can quickly become confusing. And confusion inevitably leads to data quality issues.

Here is an example of a rollout plan based on the "walk before you run" concept:

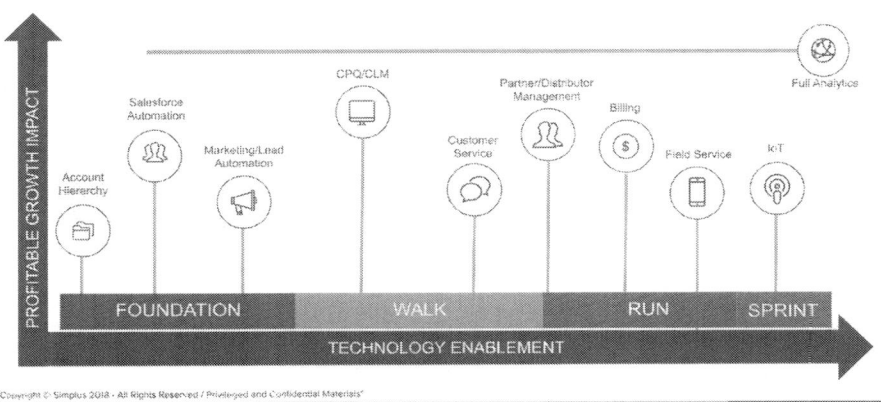

Big-Bang Rollout

By contrast, a big-bang rollout is one that hits all at once, with all departments, regions, sites, users, etc., going live at the same time. Let's consider the benefits and drawbacks of this approach:

Benefits

- **Quick Return:** With everything hitting all at once, your ROI is almost immediate.
- **Low Cost:** By doing everything at once, you naturally lower your operating expenses.

Drawbacks

- **Disruptive:** If a phased rollout is like dipping your toes in a pool, a big-bang rollout is like doing a cannonball.

The shock of the cold water is immediate, and rather than sending out ripples, you've sent out waves that threaten everyone near you. In a big-bang rollout, your organization is forced to drop everything to focus on the changes and get adjusted as quickly as possible. Your organization's productivity could suffer.

- **High Risk:** Changing everything at once is a risky move. With so many moving parts and so much rush, small details can be overlooked that can lead to bigger problems. Processes may not get the testing they need, and a problem in one area can lead to a domino effect that takes out the whole system. In the end, it may create a sink-or-swim scenario for your employees.

Although risks are higher with a big-bang rollout, such risks can be significantly reduced and mitigated with proper change management in place. Check back to chapter 8 for best practice advice in change management.

Making Your Choice

It's all about understanding and being ready for your future state. Refer back to chapter 7 and make sure you know what your future state looks like.

With either strategy, remember this: just because you can do it doesn't mean you should do it. Yes, you can do a big-bang rollout with everything you've ever dreamed about. But it will likely take you multiple years to get there. By the time you get there, your requirements will have changed. You keep refactoring without ever going live. The most successful projects are those where you start simple and progressively build and adjust the solution with each staged rollout.

Also, consider this: the decision doesn't have to be "either/ or." You can mix criteria. You can do a phased rollout on one product line in North America alone. You could do a big bang in North America first and then roll out by product line in another region.

Important Questions to Ask

Do you have the change management in place for this digital transformation?

If you go through a digital transformation, you'll go through a ton of change management to do so. As with any project of that nature, you cannot be certain that 100 percent of your future changes will be ideal. Test this digital transformation on a subset of the business using the same kind of criteria. In that case, from a digital management perspective, you want to test the whole process but on the subset of a business.

How do you get ready if you don't know if you are? Define your future state and plan for change management. Simplus can help in both areas.

Do you have the "go" from the go/no-go team?

Have you done adequate SIT and UAT testing? Like any other strategy of a quote-to-cash implementation, you need to start early. Your rollout strategy is going to impact your user stories. It impacts the prioritization of your requirements and therefore what you implement.

Do you have the executive and stakeholder buy-in?

This problem is often faced in the European market. When you're working in several countries at once, it's difficult and takes a lot of time to come up with a unified process because regulations and culture are so different from country to country. In many situations, you simply can't unify the strategy. It's not just resistance to change; sometimes, you don't have a choice. The more variables and processes you have, the more complex it will be. Because there won't be a single process for the user stories, you have to take into account corner cases, which leads to even more complexities. Again, keep in mind that edge cases do not necessarily need to be implemented, as long as you have mitigation points in place for them. A low-touch process can be acceptable when you can't reach the ideal no-touch process.

At the end of the day, your rollout strategy should be a balancing act between maximizing your ROI, time to market (project timeline and deadlines), business and team readiness, and change management maturity in your organization. Evaluate carefully the risks associated with big-bang rollout. Most companies privilege a staged rollout to minimize such risks, get some quick wins upfront, and keep the hype up about the quote-to-cash initiative.

CHAPTER THIRTEEN

INTEGRATION STRATEGY

A decade ago, the only viable way for organizations to integrate two systems was to invest in complex, custom programming to allow a bidirectional exchange of data. Most businesses could not afford to integrate their entire business ecosystem; doing so was prohibitively expensive, labor-intensive, and associated with too much risk. But times are changing, and those businesses that do not integrate are destined to fall behind.

Businesses are acutely aware of the need to better integrate their systems. One study found that 89 percent of businesses report experiencing drawbacks as a result of poor integration, even as 99 percent of businesses report recognizing the benefits of becoming more connected.[1]

In this chapter, we will discuss how to prepare for integration, how to avoid common integration mistakes, and how to select the right integration partner, then introduce key players in the industry.

Preparing for Integration

Before you can implement a QTC integration, you must determine the business strategy behind your integration—that is, how you will use your integration to drive sales and improve your customer service experience. This is a monumental task that involves tapping into the expertise, insights, and perspectives of your entire organization, including your broader ecosystem of vendors and other external partners.

Understand Business Requirements

Integration is not an IT-driven task, but rather a business-driven task. You should be spending copious time working with all of your business teams to understand what they're trying to get out of the integration and how a streamlined integration will provide the data they need to make them more efficient. It then becomes your job to either find a way to implement these specifications or to push back against unrealistic expectations. One common request from business teams that is actually quite challenging to implement is real-time data synchronization between multiple applications. Salesforce imposes governor limits designed to prevent any individual component of the system from consuming too many resources, which means that real-time integrations are notoriously difficult without a sound integration strategy. Thus, it becomes your job to balance business needs with the practical limitations of the Salesforce system.

On a side note, think carefully about an integration that you call "real time." A true real-time integration is rarely, if ever, actually needed. The real-time aspect of an integration is almost always a perception of a need, rather than an actual need. In most cases, you need access to the most current data. Such access usually does not require a real-time integration. After hundreds of QTC implementations, I have yet to find a business that can really justify a true need for real-time integration. Take this time to strategize around which specific data elements are needed by their respective parties and how quickly they really need access to this data.

Define Your Implementation Team's Roles and Responsibilities

In the middle of your implementation, the pressure will be intense, and the stakes will be high. You will need a clear delineation of responsibilities, a defined chain of command that includes a project leader, and established processes for soliciting and weighing multiple stakeholder perspectives. Your implementation team should include representatives from all major business units in your organization that will be impacted by the integration. Meanwhile, SMEs from your IT team will need to be in place to advise you on what is and isn't possible. As you begin custom development work, you'll also need a team in place to systematically conduct beta testing on the user interface, as well as perform data quality checks.

Thoroughly Clean Your Data

When other systems are integrated with Salesforce, businesses typically must develop a plan for moving data from these systems into Salesforce. Even before you plan on how to move this data, you should be developing a strategy for cleaning up your data. Perhaps you have records for products in your system that you haven't offered in years. Perhaps you have accounts from customers who haven't done business with you in a decade or more, or you have records for companies that have undergone mergers, consolidations, and name changes. Salesforce relies on clean data to work its analytical magic; thus, preparing for your integration is a perfect opportunity to do some thorough data scrubbing.

Develop a Data Migration Plan

When a business wants to move data into Salesforce from another system, it's not as simple as clicking a few buttons and then counting on Salesforce to "figure out" how to establish a continuous bidirectional sync of this data. Most businesses need a middleware tool that can read the data and manage the transfer of data into Salesforce. A middleware tool helps you architect an integration flow that is optimal for maintaining clean, accurate data over the long term.

Develop a Strategy for Transforming Your Data

Once another system has been integrated with Salesforce, you'll need to decide how the data from this system should be treated as it moves from source to destination. Importing raw data into Salesforce probably won't be useful to you; instead, you're likely to need to transform it in some manner. Perhaps you'll want to set up Salesforce Platform Events or post-process the data in Apex. No matter what data management strategy you develop, it's your job to define the steps you'll need to transform, route, approve, and otherwise manipulate your data as it moves from source to destination.

Create a Systems Integration Testing (SIT) Strategy

Once you have all of the above defined, it's now time to create your deployment strategy. Often one of the most overlooked components for an integration, this piece is critical to the success of a project. In order to ensure that the business experiences minimal downtime during a deployment, a solid testing strategy is a must! This usually requires procuring testing environments from different vendors, manufacturing test data in each application so you can run end-to-end testing scenarios, and coordinating hands-on testing time with all respective parties. Whatever your systems integration testing strategy is, make sure it is executed to the letter!

Retain an Implementation Partner

As you prepare to integrate Salesforce with other systems, your implementation team should consist of more than just your in-house experts. Any technical expert on your staff can figure out how to implement a Salesforce integration, but that doesn't mean it will be optimally configured, bug-free, and future-proofed against system updates and other changes. By contrast, an integration partner will know how to minimize risks, reduce development costs, and ensure you get the most out of your integration. For example, your integration partner will help you leverage the correct APIs as you build your Salesforce integration. If you're doing bulk updates, your integration partner will make sure you're taking full advantage of bulk updates. If caching and paging options are available, your integration partner will know how to verify that you're using all of them—and using them correctly. Ultimately, your integration partner will keep your implementation moving continuously forward and prevent you from heading down a dead-end rabbit hole or straying from best industry practices.

Businesses count on Salesforce integrations to extend the capabilities and power of the Salesforce platform. To adequately prepare for an integration, you should start by building a thorough understanding of stakeholders' requirements and priorities for the integration, define clear roles and responsibilities for the implementation team, and perform a full cleaning of the data that will be integrated. You should also develop both a data migration plan for transforming your data as it moves from source to destination and a data stewardship strategy to ensure the newly cleansed and migrated data retains its quality in both Salesforce and downstream applications. Finally, you should retain the expert services of an implementation partner that will ensure you maintain forward momentum while minimizing risks and costs.

Avoiding Common Integration Pitfalls

When you decide to invest in integrations, time is of the essence. The C-suite expects to see integrations rolled out quickly to maximize return on investment, and management commonly assumes integrations can be implemented at the same speed as QTC itself. But the process is complex. If you don't do your homework in planning for integration, you can end up with data that is misaligned, improperly transformed, and ultimately unhelpful for driving key business decisions.

Although there's no magic-bullet solution for guaranteeing the perfect integration, the single most important thing you can do is slow down and plan accordingly. The time and energy you spend at the upfront will pay off in the end. When you speed up, you run the risk of falling into entirely avoidable, cringe-worthy integration pitfalls. Let's explore six of the most common mistakes when implementing integrations and what you can do to avoid them.

Creating Shadow IT

Shadow IT consists of all of the software and systems within an organization that various individual business units have implemented without the knowledge of their IT department. Sometimes the IT department is kept intentionally in the dark, and sometimes other departments simply neglect to bring IT into the conversation. Either way, the problem is that the integration doesn't get properly developed and vetted when IT isn't consulted. Over the long term, this shadow integration may negatively impact other systems, compromise security, and fail or become glitchy. The only way to avoid creating shadow IT is to always plan your integrations alongside your IT department. You should be sharing with IT what you envision, and be deferential to them when they suggest modifications. The last thing you want is headaches down the road that could compromise the long-term integrity and security of your business ecosystem.

Introducing Too Much Customization

Every stakeholder involved in planning for an integration is likely to have very specific requests for how the configuration should be developed and configured—and they aren't likely to want to make any compromises. The challenge is that these customization requests can often take the integration further away from standard best-practices implementation and result in unnecessary complexity that makes the integration difficult to maintain and update over the long term. The only way to avoid excessive customization is to constantly push back against these customization requests and convince others to adhere to out-of-the-box functionality as much as possible. You also want to show your critics that they can still get what they want out of an integration, even if you aren't able to adhere to their exact specifications and customizations.

THE DEFINITIVE QUOTE-TO-CASH GUIDE

Overlooking Collaborations with Your Stakeholders

QTC integrations almost always prove their value to more than just the users who conceptualized and developed the integration. Once this new data and information enter the Salesforce ecosystem, it becomes suddenly accessible to every business unit inside and outside your organization, including external vendors and partners. Meanwhile, Salesforce immediately begins analyzing and parsing the data to generate insights and business intelligence. However, the way that users discover this wealth of information is almost by accident. Furthermore, once discovered, these new users immediately begin wishing the integration had been designed differently. Thus, rather than receive feedback in a reactive mode, you should be bringing all potential stakeholders to the table in a proactive manner. Not only will you get valuable input from them, but you can also share with them your implementation timeline, enabling them to plan accordingly and help minimize downtime and user confusion.

Bringing in Too Much Data

When organizations conceptualize an integration, they tend to think ambitiously about all potential related data sets that could become part of this integration project. While it may be possible to sync all of this data via an integration, it's not a smart idea. The more fields and data sources that are part of an integration, the slower and more cumbersome the integration will run. Especially when you create multiple nested objects, you risk adding unnecessary complexity. Furthermore, when you aren't selective about what data you bring in, you run the risk of end users not being able to manage all of the data over the long term. You cannot afford to have stale and obsolete data.

Postponing Addressing Access and Security Issues

A Salesforce integration often involves sending data through your internal network infrastructure. Many organizations don't think through the implications of this data routing, even though it can have significant, real-world implications. First, the data could be systematically blocked or delayed by a firewall or other security protocol. Second, the integration may expose your data to a new level of risk that your existing security systems are not designed to guard against. The best way to prevent these issues from becoming a problem is to partner with your IT department up front. You should be working with your IT department to proactively open up firewall access, and you should be testing your access controls in advance—i.e., before you're ready to begin implementation. You also should be fully investigating whether additional security measures will need to be implemented. Regulated companies especially are subject to rigid, strict data security standards; you want to ensure you'll still be in compliance with these requirements after your integration goes live.

Choosing the Wrong Tool for the Job

One of the most important decisions you'll make as you proceed through the Salesforce integration journey is what tool will facilitate the integration. Not all integration tools are created equally, and keeping in mind the company's long-term goals as well as short-term goals will determine the integration strategy's success in the long run. To do this, you'll want to research integration tools that are able to scale with your business as it grows, acquires new companies, or even as it launches new product offerings. Choosing the wrong tool could lead to the most dreaded outcome of all: technical debt. Carefully analyze the landscape before you make a commitment. Is their pricing structure able to be flexible as you scale? Do they have success stories in your industry? How will your business's long-term strategy be affected by the tool? How do they enable you to be successful? Only by asking and answering these questions will you come to the right choice on which tool is the right fit for your business.

Selecting the Right Integration Partner

When you're looking for a partner to facilitate an integration, your first inclination might be to tap the partner that helped you implement QTC itself. The best implementation partners, however, know the limits of their expertise and will likely advise you to partner with a consultant with specific expertise in doing integrations. Before you can evaluate potential integration partners, you've got to do your homework and learn what you should be evaluating in your candidates. Not only do you need to make sure your consultant is experienced and competent, but you also need to find a good match—a partner that has a track record of successfully helping clients just like you.

Find a Partner with Expertise in the Vertical

Salesforce integrations are useful in different ways to different industries and sectors. Once an integration connects two or more systems, the data can be parsed, transformed, and analyzed in any number of ways. That's why it's important to find an integration partner that has experience and expertise in your industry vertical. Whether the vertical is retail, manufacturing, healthcare, or whatever else, you should be looking for a partner that understands the pain points common in your industry and has experience applying Salesforce integrations to solve those business challenges. A partner with expertise in your vertical will be able to come to you with educated, well-researched ideas and customized, proven solutions.

Look for Creativity and Adaptability

Every organization has a unique set of systems and workflows. Thus, Salesforce integration partners cannot apply a one-size-fits-all approach to implementing integrations. In fact, the best integration partners are creative and adaptable; they understand they'll be working across multiple different products and potentially even leveraging the expertise and resources of other Salesforce partners just like them. They are distinguished by their boundless enthusiasm, flexibility, and willingness to learn and continually expand their knowledge.

Choose Partners Engaged with Their Professional Community

The Salesforce community is big, robust, and worldwide, with partners, vendors, and customers coming together in a dynamic professional community to share knowledge, insights, perspectives, and stories. The best integration partners are not only actively engaged in this community, but are regarded as leaders in the space. They participate in community panels, attend conferences and trade shows, and pen articles, blogs, and ebooks. Their involvement is not only a reflection of their dedication to bettering the Salesforce community, but also a reflection of their quest to constantly be learning and growing.

Examine the Partner's Internal Resources

No matter how passionate and experienced a Salesforce partner is, the partner also needs a critical mass of staff to support you on your implementation journey. As you evaluate integration partners, you should be looking for evidence that your prospective partner has a staff with clearly delineated roles: business analysts, consultants, admins, quality assurance checkers, and so forth. Each of these people should hold at least one Salesforce certification or certification on the integration platform. You also should be evaluating your partner's ability to provide long-term support. Once your integration is up and running, you may find that you need 24/7 support, and/or you may decide to outsource some maintenance and update responsibilities to your partner that you originally planned to do in-house. You need to understand at the upfront your implementation partner's capacity to provide these resources to you on an as-needed basis.

Look for Evidence of Technical Acumen

Every Salesforce integration partner will bring technical skills to the table. It's your job to assess the technical skills of all prospective partners to ensure you're choosing the one with a mix of skills that's ideal for your needs. As you interview consultants, you want to ask them to go into depth on how they would build your requirements, how they hand off to their developers, how they manage the preparation of client data, what their rollback or fallout procedure is, and when and how they negotiate the full project scope with their client. You also should be asking them to explain how they divvy up their roles and responsibilities to optimally serve their clients. The best integration partners will offer you detailed case studies that reveal how they successfully worked through previous, similar implementations, and how they successfully overcame challenges similar to the ones you face.

Your integration partner plays an essential role in helping you roll out an integration in an informed, strategic manner.

To ensure you select an implementation partner with an optimal combination of expertise and real-life experience, you should be looking for a partner that has expertise in the vertical, that is creative and adaptable, that is engaged actively in the broader Salesforce community, that has adequate internal resources, and that possesses rich technical acumen.

Key Players in the Industry

In a recent webinar held by Simplus, 72 percent of attendees had clients with integration needs. That number is no surprise; with any digital transformation system, you have a backend system that exists outside of the Salesforce system. For example, Salesforce doesn't support order management, fulfillment, invoicing and ERP, etc.

In Salesforce, CPQ ends at the order phase. Integration helps distribute your orders to the proper system, be it contract management, revenue recognition, order management, provisioning, shipment, inventory management, etc. That capability can often determine whether you will keep a valued customer or lose them to a competitor.

The "Who's Who" in the Integration Landscape

There are three real leaders in this space: MuleSoft, Boomi, and Informatica. MuleSoft, which was recently acquired by Salesforce, is a powerful integration platform that provides huge flexibility to the end customer, and as such is widely adopted by two of the most complicated industries: financial services and healthcare. Informatica, one of the first players in the market, is typically already entrenched in many enterprise organizations and plays a sizable role in the software/IT vertical. Finally, Dell Boomi promotes itself as a low-code, low-maintenance platform through its web interface and is a hit in the public sector. While each of these tools has its own unique platforms and benefits, we have chosen to focus on MuleSoft based on the flexibility it gives the customers to adapt to both their current and future needs.

MuleSoft is the only real player in the game that is able to support API-led connectivity, essentially creating integrations through a network of APIs. The structure design typically pairs one API to one purpose, which is fine. But, used as a vehicle for a Salesforce integration, MuleSoft's Anypoint design makes processes flexible, scalable, and manageable. In comparison to the standard API designs—which require constructing a unique API for each function—each connection with MuleSoft's Anypoint platform is reusable. Further, the platform helps create a network of pluggable assets promoting self-service tasks among team members and helps them complete projects faster. As MuleSoft's Brandon Cohan explains,

> As a result of delivering these integrations faster, the applications those integrations support are released to market faster, which has a positive impact on the business outcome (improved time-to-market).[2]

So what does this mean for you? First, this platform offers API-led connectivity. Second, MuleSoft supports on-premise, cloud, and hybrid deployment strategies. Third, MuleSoft supports DataWeave, a rich, internal development language. Finally, it provides comprehensive, interactive testing without running flow.

That means an exciting ROI for customers. In fact, in Simplus' webinar, 71 percent of attendees said they were "very likely" to use MuleSoft to integrate to CPQ.

How Does That Look in the Industry?

As your customers' needs evolve, so too does your business's need for a system catering to those needs. One report found that only 70 percent of service reps say "they can find all the information they need to do their job on one screen." Salesforce contributor Esther Chen writes,

> MuleSoft's Anypoint Platform enables organizations to synchronize data and automate transactions between Salesforce Service Cloud, ERP, and other third-party systems, whether on-premises or in the cloud.[3]

When your business needs a collaborative, responsive service just to compete in your industry, MuleSoft and Service Cloud are the perfect combination. As Chen explains, they make it easier to build that service experience and drive increased customer satisfaction and new revenue streams.

And don't forget the matter of scalability. As your business grows, your work system must be able to accommodate that growth.

As you tackle integration, the most important things are that you (1) not rush into things and (2) be sure to get the right help. Put in the time preparing for integration, identify and avoid common integration mistakes, select the right integration partner, and follow the lead of the industry's key players.

CHAPTER FOURTEEN

MAINTAINING YOUR QTC SOLUTION

Maintaining your QTC solution alone can be a huge burden. The landscape is constantly shifting, meaning that you can't simply install and then forget about your solution. Even as it saves you time and money, your solution will need constant maintenance to ensure you get the most out of it, enhancing it whenever the opportunity presents itself.

Accept now that you won't be able to hit the ground running. Maintaining your QTC solution is not without pain points. However, find the right answer to those pain points, and your solution will run seamlessly and yield the results you've worked so hard thus far to achieve.

Pain Points

As you approach maintaining your QTC solution, you'll doubtless encounter some pain points standing in your way. Here are three of the most common.

1. Not Having a Full Skill Set Internally

The simple fact is that your business isn't filled with QTC experts. Now, I firmly believe that anyone can become an expert, so long as they have the time to put in the work and the drive to do so. However, asking your employees to achieve that rank may be asking too much, especially when they'd much rather dedicate time to the work they were hired to do. And paying for the training for enough of your employees to make a difference is an expensive endeavor as well.

2. Not Having the Budget to Hire the Internal Resources

The most obvious answer to the previous pain point is to simply hire people with the needed skill set. Many companies hire an in-house employee or small team of Salesforce specialists to help maintain their QTC solution.

Hiring and retaining Salesforce resources can be costly for an organization. According to Glassdoor, the United States' national average salaries to hire these as internal resources are significant: for example, a Salesforce administrator and developer can each cost upwards of $87K, while an integration specialist can run over $101K.[1] Compounding the cost is the fact that the average tenure in these jobs is less than two years!

3. Needing Maintenance to Run on Autopilot While the Internal Team Focuses Elsewhere

At the beginning of this chapter, your eyes may have bugged out a bit when you read "constant maintenance." You didn't pick up this book because you wanted a new responsibility on top of your current ones; you're not looking for new tasks that eat up valuable time better spent on the work you're passionate about. You are interested in QTC for what it can do to assist your business—*not* to distract from it. All this means that you need a solution that can run on autopilot while you and your team focus your attention elsewhere.

Managed Services

In light of all we've discussed thus far, there is only one option that answers all of your needs and offers you escape from every pain point: hiring a consultancy firm to provide managed services for your QTC solution. Managed services save you the time, money, and worry of constantly hiring in-house admins and developers. Plus, you get more expertise and skill sets than you would with one in-house staff member working on your QTC instance. Here are just some of the benefits of hiring external managed services.

Access a Broad Range of Expertise

Despite the allure of having your own Salesforce specialist or team working in-house, you're limiting yourself to a specific skill set or small collection of Salesforce knowledge. In that respect, a Salesforce consultancy firm clearly comes out on top, as you benefit from the skills of hundreds of experts—everything from success managers to system admins, business analysts to operations experts.

Leave Behind Tribal Knowledge

In response to the high level of competition in the Salesforce ecosystem, in-house consultants are highly mobile—they're always on the lookout for better opportunities and will leave as soon as a better position opens up elsewhere. When they leave, they're taking all of their tribal knowledge with them. When you hire an outside consultancy, though, you're never at risk of losing that knowledge, as it's shared among hundreds of experts.

Easily Predict Costs

In-house professionals are a fixed cost. That means that, regardless of the work being done, you're obligated to pay salary as well as other expenses such as healthcare, taxes, and other benefits. But that may not be reflective of how active they are. For example, one week may be busy, requiring hours of work changing, maintaining, or implementing components or services to keep your users happy. But the next week or weeks could be dead quiet. An outside consultant would then be the preferred option, as they can provide blended rates and adjust their capacity without incurring additional costs.

Gain a Subjective Perspective

Hiring in-house means limiting your perspective to the opinions, experience, and expertise of the one or few you hire. Outside consultancies, however, can afford to be subjective in their judgment. They have experience from working on dozens or hundreds of similar projects from which to draw and can pick their colleagues' brains to find the best solution.

Make Decisions That Will Last

The Salesforce environment is constantly changing and improving. Outside consultants are often privileged to inside information on future releases of Salesforce, which can impact solution architecture.

When moving forward with your QTC solution, the best option available to you is to hire a consultancy firm to provide managed services. Doing so will answer your pain points, ensuring your solution functions optimally and uninterrupted.

.

CHAPTER FIFTEEN

BEST PRACTICES FOR YOUR QTC JOURNEY

If you have read through this book thus far, you understand that QTC is a complex and long journey and that it evolves constantly as your company grows over time. It's time to take a step back and put things in perspective. This chapter shares valuable tips and best practices that you should keep in mind as you progress through the four stages of your quote-to-cash journey: evaluate, plan, implement, and maintain.

Stage 1: Evaluate

In the evaluate stage, your primary goal is to take stock of all of the options available to you in terms of solutions, partners, methodologies, and budget.

PROJECT STARTING POINTS

Key Considerations

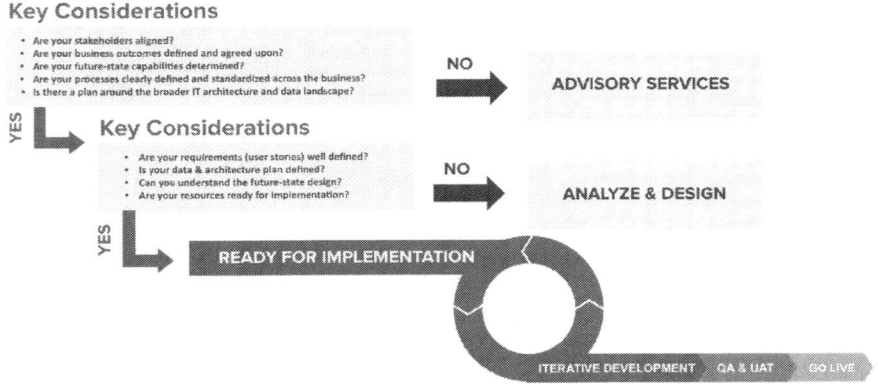

Choosing a Flexible Solution

Obviously, the first part of the evaluation is choosing the technology platform for CPQ, CLM, and billing. If you elect to purchase an off-the-shelf solution, your primary technology objective should be a flexible solution with low code, therefore reducing the technical debt for your future state and making it easier to implement future product upgrades. This will also provide you with maximum flexibility when it comes to enhancing your solution as your business evolves over time. Furthermore, if you embrace the concepts presented in chapter 12, you will be facing constant evolution as you progressively realize the future state for your company. Being able to push new enhancements and functionality with the highest agility will be very important for your long-term ROI.

Choosing a Partner

Even more important than the platform itself is the choice of the right partner to help you through this journey. As you have understood through this book, QTC is a complex process with many subtleties in terms of user stories. Optimizing your processes and implementing the tools correctly requires a deep level of expertise in both of these areas, but also with downstream processes and integration.

Experience in this domain is key. Do not hesitate to ask potential partners for references. Check peer reviews on specialized sites such as the AppExchange or G2. Has your future partner sufficient expertise in your industry or market segment? What challenges did other customers face when working with such partner and such technology platform? Is this partner trusted by the technology vendor? Do they have the right set of certifications? Are they a proven expert for the QTC platform you have chosen?

Implementation Methodology

As we learned earlier in chapter 9, QTC projects are different. The best method is a hybrid approach. They require a thorough analysis and design phase and benefit most from an iterative build phase before following a traditional QA and deployment final phase. Make sure you choose a partner that promotes the use of a hybrid methodology and commit to that methodology yourself.

Budget

Make sure you consider more than just the price of the licenses to use the tools. Evaluate the price of working with a partner and the expertise they will bring to the table. QTC is a dynamic but long-term investment—you want to pick wisely from the start.

Stage 2: Plan

Once you've evaluated all of your options, the time has come to start planning. The majority of your attention will go towards ensuring that your organization can handle what is to come and prepping your people for the work ahead.

Break Your Project into Phases

Don't try to boil the ocean. QTC is a journey!

As mentioned in chapter 7, it is important to know what you want to do in the long term. To maximize your chances of reaching this future state, start simple and introduce more and more functionality in the solution over the months, through multiple releases and launches.

The most successful projects are those where the stakeholders have been able to ruthlessly prioritize their requirements. Focus on the big immediate wins around common user stories to resolve your most important pain points and start automating your processes. Being able to quickly deliver some ROI early on will also help keep your executives' buy-in.

Finally, use mitigation points (such as approvals) for edge cases.

Revisit chapter 12 to refresh your memory on how to prioritize and drive your project team to work on what is most valuable for your business.

Avoid a "Lift and Shift"

For those of you using an existing QTC solution and wanting to replace it, do not try to mimic what that prior system was doing. You will most likely fail!

Changing a critical system such as CPQ or billing is a perfect opportunity to rethink, optimize, and unify your processes. As you go through this thought process, keep the following key objectives in mind:

- Identify and apply best practices.
- Thrive for simplification.
- Remain consistent.
- Automate as much as you can.

Clean Up Your Data

Most modern systems make extensive use of reference data, also called master data. This data is easily manipulated by your system administrators and is consumed by different rules engines.

This exercise goes way beyond deduplicating accounts and contacts! In order to take full advantage of powerful CPQ capabilities, for example, you will have to revisit the following:

- Rationalize the structure of the product catalog, having flexible bundling and kitting in mind.
- Reevaluate complex pricing models such as attribute-based pricing and dynamic pricing, and company policies in terms of system-driven discounts.
- Eliminate price book proliferation, as CPQ can easily handle multichannel and multimarket sales scenario.

This is a must for accuracy and automation!

Get Your Team Ready

Because of their nature, QTC projects should be driven by the business, not by your IT department. As such, you need to identify a business executive sponsor as early as possible.

Reach out deep into your organization to list all relevant sales and product experts (subject matter experts, or SMEs) and prepare them for their future mission of supporting the project. Don't forget experts in finance, legal, sales ops, and downstream processes such as fulfillment, revenue recognition, commission calculations, and so on. These stakeholders will all have significant value to bring on the table for the future solution you are about to build.

Finally, make sure your IT team will have the proper resources to enable the implementation. They will have a critical role in dealing with master data, legacy data migrations, and integration points between systems.

If you lack in-house resources in some of these areas, identify a partner who can bring such expertise for a successful outcome.

Document the Requirements

This might seem obvious, but this is overlooked more often than not. Every business can work on defining their requirements, at least at a high level, before the implementation project starts. Make the important decisions early on so that the teams can keep a strong momentum during the entire project. Too many times, the project gets stalled because the stakeholders can't come up with the difficult decisions in a timely manner.

If you have carefully defined your future state, you should already be in pretty good shape. If not, start with your product catalog and what it should look like when you think about selling a solution to your end customers instead of selling individual products and services. As part of this process, you will necessarily deal with product dependencies, product filtering and selection, guided selling, and guided configuration concepts.

Think about selling value instead of selling price. This will help you link product catalog structure with pricing models. This will also help you define edge cases and what approval authorities should be involved in the process.

Finally, this will allow you to reflect on how to incorporate your brand in the generated quote documents that your end customers will accept and sign. This document should be looked at as a powerful selling tool, sending a strong and clear message to maximize deal close rates. Ultimately, your end customers must understand immediately

- what they buy from you,
- why they buy it,
- for what kind of value, and
- at what price.

Proceed with a similar exercise when it comes to CLM or billing:

- What should the contract lifecycle look like in your organization?
- What key elements of a contract are negotiated and should be tracked?
- What are the key constraints involved in billing and invoicing?
- What should happen to ensure a low- or no-touch billing process?
- How will you go from invoicing to payment collection and accounts receivable management?

Legacy Data Migration

Don't overlook the importance of legacy data migration. The quote-to-cash process starts with CPQ. CPQ controls the overall contract lifecycle. Therefore, it is critical that CPQ be able to consume data from your install base, which is defined by the prior purchases made by your customers. This concept is absolutely critical in a subscription-based business model.

I highly recommend that you consider your needs for legacy data migration as part of your planning process. You can define the general criteria without knowing how the future CPQ platform works or its exact data model:

- **Cut-off Criteria:** You only need to migrate products and services that are currently "active" with your customers.
- **Source Systems:** Know where the current information resides and how much is available as structured vs. unstructured data.

A similar analysis will be required in CLM and billing:

- Where is your current contract repository? Is it made of structured or unstructured data?
- What is the cut-off date for your billing implementation?
- Where will you collect the A/R balance or in-flight invoices and payments?
- Who are the current experts in maintaining such data in external systems?

Change Management

I will never say it enough: change management is critical for the success of your QTC journey!

Here are the key elements you need to plan for:

- Start shaping your rollout plan. Think about how you will deploy the solution throughout the organization, as this requires you to start prioritizing early on.
- Think about adoption from the onset, identify future champion users, and get their early participation.

Technology is the easy part. Aligning people and processes is the hard part.

Stage 3: Implement

Finally, the time has come to implement! It's an exciting time—one you've been working towards—so be sure not to rush it. Here are some things to consider.

Source of Truth

Choose a source of truth for each set of reference data and rules:

- Customer master
- Product master
- Pricing master
- Order master

The source can be different for each set of data. But it must be consistent to avoid creating unnecessary complexities.

This will also help you identify integration points between systems.

Design Inside the Box

When you purchase off-the-shelf software solutions, you must consider that such solutions will cover most of your needs. Otherwise, you would have chosen to build the tool from scratch.

Off-the-shelf packages implement many common patterns in business processes and support them out of the box. Therefore, you should keep your design "inside the box" and avoid customizations when you can. However, don't fear customizations! When it comes to Salesforce CPQ, for example, use the many different plugins available in the CPQ platform to your advantage. Many design and implementation patterns have well-documented solutions by using such plugins. I call them "standard customizations." Do not hesitate to write a few lines of code in a plugin if this code replaces a complex and large set of declarative rules. You will gain clarity and ease of maintenance of your solution.

The use of out-of-the-box functionality contributes to reducing the "accumulated engineering debt" and facilitates release upgrades.

Avoid Complexity

Complexity is usually manufactured: you always have the choice of keeping things simple. It is human nature to overthink or overengineer. Always focus on the 20 percent of requirements that address 80 percent of your business needs.

Strongly resist the temptation to implement edge cases! Going for the last 5 percent can negatively impact the performance or outcome of the first 95 percent. Think mitigation controls.

QTC projects are a special kind of breed, especially when it comes to CPQ: it is highly recommended to adapt your processes to the capabilities of the tools you have chosen, rather than the reverse, even though this might seem counterintuitive at first.

Stage 4: Manage

Your job doesn't end with implementation. Going forward, you need to manage what you've set in place.

Deployment Process

QTC journeys are living creatures and constantly evolve as the needs of your business change. You will introduce new products and services, and change your processes based on new market conditions or business context, such as mergers and acquisitions. As a result, your implemented solution will be in constant evolution.

Make sure you put a flexible process in place to deploy changes on a regular basis from one environment to the next: sandbox to sandbox, and ultimately to your production instance.

Remember that QTC solutions rely heavily on reference data, which is hard to deploy correctly. Don't hesitate to use specialized tools such as Prodly Moover.

With a staged rollout strategy, and within each stage of the rollout through an iterative build as recommended with the hybrid implementation methodology, you will have to deploy your solution on a frequent basis. Having a structured approach to using different environments is important: one or several development environments (one per major internal project, for example) will deploy into a UAT or testing environment. You might have a separate training instance as well to train your end users before a major rollout. And finally, a full staging environment containing an exact copy of the next version of your production instance allows you to deploy more safely into your critical, live systems.

The more you can automate this deployment process, the faster you can go to market with new functionality and enhancements to your solutions. Your users will greatly appreciate it.

Success Metrics

Quote-to-cash projects are unique in that they are very transformational projects and involve almost every conceivable aspect of your organization. Many stakeholders will participate and provide different opinions, which will pull you in different directions. Make sure you keep your true north and focus on the low-hanging fruits and delivering business value and great ROI. Remember that it's a journey: it does not end with the first go-live—rather, it begins with it.

Identify and define your success criteria early on, based on the expected ROI. Always remember WHY you are doing this to prioritize strategically.

Solution Ownership

As much as possible, take ownership of the solution delivered by your implementation partner. Do not hesitate to invest in a Salesforce administrator with knowledge and expertise in QTC.

If you can't or don't want to invest in an in-house administrator, go with a proven managed service provider with strong expertise in QTC who can handle ongoing maintenance of the master data—such as new product launches or price changes and promotions handling—as well as implement new features from suggestions collected from your end users.

Or go with both types of resources! While your own administrator helps on the next phase and rollout of the solution, use a managed service provider to maintain the current implementation.

Regardless of your approach, remember that there is nothing more potentially dangerous than having someone with no experience or expertise attempting to make regular updates and changes to your implemented solution.

Creating Hype

Hype up the new system! Get everyone excited about it, from users to executives. Take advantage of a major company event such as a sales kick-off to announce it. Make a presentation with a sneak peek of the future system or even organize a live demo, showing users how it will help resolve their current problems.

Use strong messaging techniques with clear explanations and emphasize the "why" to maximize the buy-in.

CONCLUSION

And there you have it. All of quote-to-cash, wrapped up in a single package. All of the general knowledge we have has been laid out for you in these pages.

But here's the thing: your business is anything but "general." It's unique. The goals you set and the challenges you face are specific to you, your market, your industry, etc. And if you've read this book and still feel overwhelmed, that's natural.

That's why Simplus is here to help. Simplus is a Platinum Salesforce Partner and provider of quote-to-cash implementations. We provide enterprise-wide digital transformation through advisory, implementation, change management, custom configuration, and managed services. Guided by the mantra, "success simplified," we use leading cloud solutions to help companies achieve a strategic vision, improve performance, and increase value to stakeholders. With more than 2,000 customers and a high customer-satisfaction rating, Simplus helps companies improve, innovate, and grow.

So come to us with your problems. Come with your questions. We can't wait to see you through to success.

For more information, please visit www.simplus.com.

ACKNOWLEDGMENTS

Over the past two decades, I have dedicated my professional life to helping others bridge the gap between business processes and technology. I have been lucky, along the way, to find great mentors on my journey. This book is one of many ways I try to pay forward the experience and wisdom I have acquired over the years.

This adventure would not have been possible without the input from all clients and coworkers I have interacted with through hundreds of projects. Not only did such interaction teach me most of what I know about quote-to-cash, but the people I interacted with are the foundation of my passion for this space. You are too many to name individually, but you know who you are! Our paths have crossed, sometimes over and over! I am forever grateful and thankful for the positive influence you have had on me.

I want to extend special thanks to Max Rudman and Godard Abel, not only for your foreword to this book, but more importantly for being great mentors and teachers for so many years. As entrepreneurs who deeply care for your employees and your clients, you built exceptional companies, and I am infinitely grateful that you allowed me to be a part of your success.

I would like to thank Ryan Westwood and Isaac Westwood, who welcomed me into the Simplus family and allowed me to continue pursuing my search for excellence in quote-to-cash. The growing team you have put together is tremendously talented and gives me the opportunity to better myself every day.

Special thanks to the many Simplus team members who contributed their time and knowledge to make the content of this book even better. Specifically, I'd like to thank Randy West on revenue recognition, Sean Ralph on billing, Mike Lockert on the sales process, Marcy Chanin on implementation methodology, Carlos Montejo on change management, Meryl Flynn and Jamie Teasdale on CLM, Ryan Northington on managed services, and Christian Tooley on integrations. My thanks also go to David Belove from Prodly for his wisdom on deployment best practices. You are all amazing!

I never imagined that writing a book would be such a complex and lengthy process. I have been blessed to be helped by the fantastic marketing team at Simplus, namely Sam Wright, Katherine Albiston, and Makenzie Clawson. Your contribution to this effort means a lot to me, from proofreading to content editing to graphical design! Thank you for your patience over the months and for your professional expertise to make this journey easier on me.

Last but not least, I would like to thank Amy Cook, chief marketing officer at Simplus. Thank you for making a simple idea come to life, for keeping me on the hook, and for guiding me through this process. Most importantly, thank you for being such a great friend!

The road to successful quote-to-cash is difficult because it includes many complex moving parts involving a large number of parallel tracks. Whether you are starting your quote-to-cash journey or you are well into it, I hope this book has given you an opportunity to take a different look at your own journey and contributed to making you more successful.

Gilles Muys

NOTES

Chapter 1 – CPQ

1. Danny Wong, "What the Future Looks Like for Configure, Price, Quote (CPQ)," Salesforce Blog, accessed October 24, 2019, https://www.salesforce.com/products/cpq/resources/future-of-configure-price-quote/.

2. Dan Lindsey, "Why A Lack Of Pricing Consistency Damages Your Brand," *Forbes*, October 23, 2017, https://www.forbes.com/sites/forbesbusinessdevelopmentcouncil/2017/10/23/why-a-lack-of-pricing-consistency-damages-your-brand/#505079816233.

3. "Case study: Helping Centrify with an overhaul of product structure," Simplus blog, accessed October 24, 2019, https://www.simplus.com/25939-2/.

4. "Breaking the Laws of Physics: Shortening the Last Sales Mile through Workflow Automation," Aberdeen Group, April 2013, https://www.determine.com/uploads/resource-pdfs/Selectica_AberdeenLeadToWin.pdf.

5. Ibid.

6. Ibid.

7. Michael Bauer, "How CPQ Software Can Get You Seeing Dollar Signs," Axonom Inc., October 9, 2015, https://www.axonom.com/how-cpq-software-can-get-you-seeing-dollar-signs.

8. Salesforce, FY20 B2B Sales Report, 2019, https://www.salesforce.com/form/conf/cpq/report-b2b-sales/?leadcreated=true&redirect=true&chapter=&DriverCampaignId=70130000000sUVq&player=&FormCampaignId=7010M0000021QScQAM&videoId=&playlistId=&mcloudHandlingInstructions=&landing_page=.

9. Ibid.

10. Salesforce, "What is Configure, Price, Quote (CPQ)?" Salesforce Blog, accessed October 24, 2019, https://www.salesforce.com/products/cpq/resources/what-is-cpq/.

11. Salesforce, "Salesforce: Sales Cloud Overview Demo," Salesforce Blog, accessed October 24, 2019, https://www.salesforce.com/form/conf/demo-sales/?leadcreated=true&redirect=true&chapter=&DriverCampaignId=70130000002IBwv&player=&FormCampaignId=7010M000002MJQ0&videoId=&playlistId=&mcloudHandlingInstructions=&landing_page=

12. Ibid.

13. Ibid.

14. Ibid.

Chapter 2 – CLM

1. Conga, *Creating a Case for Contract Management in Healthcare*, 2018, https://getconga.com/wp-content/uploads/eBook_Legal_Healthcare.pdf.

2. Simplus, "Seamless contract management with SpringCM and Simplus," Simplus Blog, accessed October 24, 2019, https://www.simplus.com/contract-management-springcm/.

3. Gartner Glossary, s.v. "Contract Life Cycle Management (clm)," accessed October 24, 2019, https://www.gartner.com/en/information-technology/glossary/contract-life-cycle-management-clm.

4. Pierce Smith, "Contract management statistics for sales leaders," SpringCM, accessed October 24, 2019, https://www.springcm.com/blog/contract-management-statistics-for-sales-leaders.

5. SpringCM, 2017 *State of Contract Management Report*, https://www.springcm.com/research-report-2017-state-of-contract-management-lp.

Chapter 3 – Billing

1. Owen Gough, "Half of businesses admit to paying suppliers late," SmallBusiness.co.uk, January 25, 2018, https://smallbusiness.co.uk/businesses-suppliers-late-payments-2542443/.

Chapter 4 – Sales Cycle

1. Academy of Achievement, "John Wooden Biography — Academy of Achievement," last modified April 27, 2018, https://www.achievement.org/achiever/john-wooden/#profile.

2. Herb Weisbaum, "Quality service, not low prices, creates loyalty," June 24, 2014, https://www.cnbc.com/2014/06/24/quality-service-not-low-prices-creates-loyalty.html.

Chapter 6 – Revenue Recognition

1. FRS 15 Revenue from Contracts with Customers, IFRS, accessed October 24, 2019. https://www.ifrs.org/issued-standards/list-of-standards/ifrs-15-revenue-from-contracts-with-customers/

2. "70% of Companies May Miss New Revenue Recognition Standard Deadline," CPA Practice Advisor, June 7, 2017, https://www.cpapracticeadvisor.com/accounting-audit/news/12341992/70-of-companies-may-miss-new-revenue-recognition-standard-deadline.

Chapter 8 – Change Management

1. Kate Leggett, "CRM Success Requires Focus On People, Not Only Technology," Forrester, February 18, 2016, https://go.forrester.com/blogs/16-02-18-crm_success_requires_focus_on_people_not_only_technology/.

2. Prosci, "Highlights and trends from the Prosci 2018 Best Practices Report," SlideShare, April 23, 2018, https://www.slideshare.net/ProsciANZ/highlights-and-trends-from-the-prosci-2018-best-practices-report.

3. Jean-Baptiste Minchelli, "6 Best Practices for Driving End-User Adoption of Salesforce," Salesforce, August 19, 2016, https://www.salesforce.com/blog/2016/08/driving-end-user-adoption-of-salesforce.html.

4. Brian Berns, "Driving User Adoption: Making Sure Your Employees Are Engaged Users," Forbes, June 30, 2017, https://www.forbes.com/sites/forbestechcouncil/2017/06/30/driving-user-adoption-making-sure-your-employees-are-engaged-users/#6e17b5b64c1a.

5. Simplus, "Mitsubishi Electric Automotive America: Knowing the customer with Sales Cloud," accessed October 24, 2019, https://www.simplus.com/mitsubishi-electric-automotive-customer/.

6. Salesforce, "Use these Four Tactics to Successfully Change Organizational Behavior," accessed October 24, 2019, https://www.salesforce.com/hub/business/improve-change-organizational-behavior/.

7. Prosci, "What is the ADKAR Model?" accessed October 24, 2019, https://www.prosci.com/adkar/adkar-model.

Chapter 10 – QA Strategy

1. *International Association of Milk Dealers, Proceedings of the ... Annual Convention* 24, no. 4 (2009): 32

Chapter 12 – Rollout Strategy

1. Salesforce, "Hitachi Vantara drives digital transformation — starting with a new recurring-revenue model," Salesforce Customer Success Stories, accessed October 24, 2019, https://www.salesforce.com/customer-success-stories/hitachi-vantara/

Chapter 13 – Integration Strategy

1. Boomi, "The Connected Business: Improving integration and creating connectivity in 2018," accessed October 25, 2019, https://boomi.com/wp-content/uploads/Dell-Boomi-and-Vanson-Bourne-The-Connected-Business-whitepaper.pdf.

2. Brandon Cohan, "Calculating the value of API-led integration," MuleSoft Blog, August 14, 2019, https://blogs.muleSoft.com/biz/connectivity/calculating-value-api-led-integration/.

3. Esther Chen, "Deliver a connected service experience with MuleSoft and Salesforce," MuleSoft Blog, May 30, 2019, https://blogs.muleSoft.com/biz/connectivity/connected-service-experience-mulesoft-salesforce/.

Chapter 14 – Maintaining Your QTC Solution

1. Glassdoor, "Salesforce Administrator Salaries in United States," accessed October 24, 2019, https://www.glassdoor.

com/Salaries/us-salesforce-administrator-salary-SRCH_IL.0,2_IN1_KO3,27.htm; Glassdoor, "Salesforce Developer Salaries in United States," accessed October 24, 2019, https://www.glassdoor.com/Salaries/us-salesforce-developer-salary-SRCH_IL.0,2_IN1_KO3,23. htm; and Glassdoor, "Integration Architect Salaries in United States," accessed October 24, 2019, https://www. glassdoor.com/Salaries/us-integration-architect-salary-SRCH_IL.0,2_IN1_KO3,24.htm.

Made in the USA
Coppell, TX
07 February 2020